HEADQUARTERS, ARMY GROUND FORCES
Army War College
Washington 25, D. C.

319.1/187(Foreign Observer)(R)   23 June 1945.
  (23 Jun 45)GNGBI

SUBJECT: Combat Lessons Gained from Overseas Observations.

TO: Commanding Generals,
      All Armies,
      All Separate Corps.

    1.   The inclosed report consists of extracts from many sources bearing on the overseas experiences of various individuals and units. A glance at the Quick Readers Index will indicate portions of primary interest to staff sections, arms and services.

    2.   There is no objection to reproduction of the entire report, or any part thereof, for subordinate units.

    3.   Data and recommendations contained in this report represent the views of the individuals concerned and are furnished for information only.

    4.   Changes in training doctrine as enunciated in War Department publications which are necessary because of the information contained in observers' reports will be published by the War Department. Changes in training directives of this headquarters which are necessary because of information in observers' reports will be promulgated by this headquarters.

    5.   This report is for distribution to units at the time of assignment or attachment to your command for administration and training for redeployment as follows:

          Each Corps   - 3
          Each Division   -25
          Each Brigade   -10
          Each Gp Hq   -10
          Each Sep Regt   - 2
          Each Sep Bn (Sq)- 1

      BY COMMAND OF MAJOR GENERAL CHRISTIANSEN:

                        R.A.Meredith

                        R. A. MEREDITH
                        Lt Col, AGD
                        Asst Ground Adjutant General

1 Incl:
  Rpt as listed in
  par 1, above.

Published by Books Express Publishing
Copyright © Books Express, 2011
ISBN 978-1-78039-510-4

Books Express publications are available from all good retail and online booksellers. For
publishing proposals and direct ordering please contact us at: info@books-express.com

DISTRIBUTION

AGF UNITS
Armies	500
Separate Corps	100
A/B Center	3
AA Comd	5
Armd Center	5
R&SC	2
TDC	4
Schools (Except TD 1)	5
1st Hq & Hq Det Sp Trps, AGF	5
All Hq & Hq Dets Sp Trps	2

OTHERS
C&GSS	5
AWC Records	1

QUICK READERS REPORT

Subject	Page	G-1	G-2	G-3	G-4	Engr	Med	Ord	Chem	QM	Sig	Inf	Arty	Cav	Armd & TD
Japanese Warfare as seen by US Observers	1	X	X	X	X							X	X	X	X
Japanese Psychology	9	X	X	X								X	X	X	X
Prisoner of War Interrogation Report	25		X	X									X		
Report on Cavalry Rcn. Sq., Mecz.	37		X	X										X	
Battle Patrol	39		X	X								X		X	
Elimination of Noise in River Crossings	40		X	X		X						X			
Report on Prisoner of War Raid	40		X											X	
Mopping up Operation, Admiralty Islands	40		X	X								X	X		
Small Unit Tactics used by Japs at Night	43		X	X								X	X	X	X
Souvenir Hunting is still a Problem	47		X					X				X	X	X	X
Operation of a Div. CIC Detachment	48		X												
Reconnaissance Troop, Liberation of Guam	51		X	X								X		X	
Field Artillery Notes	56			X									X		
Tank-Infantry Operation	57			X								X			X
War Dogs	62			X		X						X		X	
Maps and Photomaps used during Amp. Opr.	72		X	X	X							X	X	X	X
Staff Inspection of Const. Activities	75				X	X									
Statements of Observers on CWS Matters	78				X				X						
Signal Communications Hollandia Operation	80		X	X	X						X				
Amphibious Supply	89			X	X					X					
Ordnance Subjects	89				X			X							
Engineer Subjects	93				X	X									
Medical Subjects	100				X		X								
Signal Subjects	118				X						X				
CIC in Italy	120		X												
CIC Operations on Leyte	122		X												

JAPANESE WARFARE AS SEEN BY U.S. OBSERVERS

1. Introduction:

The comments carried in this section are made by observers, who have been in the Southwest Pacific theater of operations, and by officers and enlisted men who have participated in the actual fighting. The comments have been edited to eliminate repetition and, as far as possible, to arrange the information according to subject matter.

2. The Japanese Soldier:

"In my opinion, the Japanese soldier is a well-trained, well-equipped and well-disciplined fighting man. He is in good physical condition, is infinitely patient and shows a sacrificial devotion to duty. The Japanese is only a fair small-arms shot, but is proficient in the use of mortars and artillery. He uses large quantities of hand grenades.

Japanese soldiers have been trained to create fear in the hearts of their opponents and they exploit to the utmost the advantage gained thereby. Although they prefer to conduct the offensive on a dark night or just at dawn, they have fallen far short of mastering the technique of night fighting.

The individual soldier is an expert camoufleur, well-trained in the most effective use of natural camouflage materials. He does a large amount of close-in fighting, but is not exceptionally proficient in the use of the bayonet or in hand-to-hand combat. He is not endowed with superhuman qualities.

The greatest weakness of the Japanese fighting man is his inability to cope effectively with unexpected situations. Although he is a very efficient cog in a war machine and follows a definite plan even to minute details, he is sorely lacking in resourcefulness and ready adaptability to rapidly changing situations. No amount of training can remedy this defect of the Japanese soldier; it is an inherent weakness which is at least partly the result of having led a closely regimented life in which free thinking and individual initiative have been discouraged. This weakness is apparent both in offensive and defensive situations. When attacking, the Japanese soldier makes extensive use of weird, piercing shrieks and of threatening cries such as "Marine, you die". The obvious intent of this practice is to demoralize his opponent and also to boost his own morale. The result expected is a disorderly, confused flight to the rear. When, however, the Japanese soldier's opponent holds his ground unwaveringly, even in the face of heavy casualties, the Jap himself becomes disorganized and confused and is then quite vulnerable to a counterattack. If, after being repulsed in the initial attack, he decides to try again, he will probably employ identical tactics.

The Japanese's well established custom of preparing his evening meal just after dusk and his morning meal at dawn offers an opportunity for catching him in known bivouac areas with concentrated artillery fire.

Our troops should understand that the Japanese is no better able to go without food than we are, but his stamina is no better than our own (provided we have taken the necessary steps to insure top physical condition), that the Jap gets just as wet when it rains and that he suffers just as much, if not more, from malaria, dysentery, dengue, ringworm and other forms of tropical ills. This has been amply borne out by the condition of prisoners captured in this area and by finding of dead who had literally starved to death.

To the Japanese, machines of war – from the heavy machine guns to the tank – are only incidentals in warfare. We Americans realize that the infantry must perform the tasks of actually taking over the ground and holding it but we use every available machine of war to prevent unnecessary losses. In contrast, the Japanese do not conceive of substituting the shock action of war machines for the shock action of infantry and they merely strengthen the shock action of troops by the assistance of the machines. The Japanese Army is an army of men, supported by machines of war; ours is an army using machines of war. This is a fine distinction and perhaps not readily understood but every statement of Japanese military policy bears this out.

A Japanese who has not tasted defeat will attack with a dash and a magnificent disregard for himself. When he has been set back on his heels, just once, he loses that zip and comes back without confidence and impelled by a morbid feeling toward death that might be worded as "Come on, let's get it over with".

He has found himself up against things he can't understand; for example, the way we use artillery (the Chinese never used it against him like that and he doesn't know what to do about it); the fact that we prefer to sit back and stop him with well aimed rifle and machine gun fire and not fight it out with the bayonet; the fact that when we meet him with a bayonet we don't break and run; and above all, the fact that his basic idea – that skill, bravery and cold steel alone will win the war – is wrong.

3. Offense:

a. During the Day.

On gaining contact along a road or trail in jungle country, Japanese forces in New Guinea usually followed a certain pattern of tactics.

First, the commander rapidly advanced specially selected, trained and equipped troops who corresponded to our advance guard.

When these forward troops gained contact with the opposition they took up a position astride the road or track and endeavored to pin down the opposing forces with the support of machine guns and mortar fire.

Next, these forward troops used various ruses and demonstrations in an attempt to scare the opposition into a withdrawal, or into revealing the strength extent and location of their position by premature movement and firing.

If our troops did not withdraw, Japanese elements in rear of their forward group tried to by-pass our positions by infiltrating or stalking around one or both flanks as speedily as possible.

A stalk is carried out by a chain of men moving by a series of sidesteps. The sidesteps are made quickly and between steps, bodies are motionless as statues and eyes are glued on the objective. Fire is opened only when a target is seen.

These forward Japanese groups can usually be easily disposed of if our troops withhold their fire until a suitable target presents itself. There are numerous instances when Japanese advance elements were permitted to pass by and the larger rear elements were accounted for by rifle or machine-gun fire.

Upon first contact (in New Guinea), the Japanese would site a machine gun behind cover and fire along the track or road. This gun usually was well protected by riflemen and difficult to dislodge. The primary mission of this group was to protect and aid the advances of their forward group, but they periodically tested the strength and location of their opposition by feints and by deliberate attack.

They made feints and rapid advances, affording just fleeting glimpses in order to draw the fire of our troops and thus determine our location and strength. By firing at these fleeting targets, our troops would immediately draw a heavy return fire by a group which was placed for that purpose.

To test the possibility of further advance, the Japanese would send men forward along the track or road under cover of fire from rifles, machine guns and mortars. They placed much confidence in the effect of sound and apparently did considerable firing for this reason.

—————   —————

If the Japanese fail in their first attempt on a position, they seem to bring their forward lines right up to within 50 yards of ours wherever possible. (Hence the importance of being able to dig in).

In many instances, the Japanese have not hesitated to send troop elements into areas where it was next to impossible to secure their return or even to supply them. As a result, some of the deep infiltrations of their troops failed because of food shortages.

Unless fields of fire have been cut, it is almost impossible to stop Japanese infiltration through jungle.

If you are assigned to do some sniping, you should first seek concealment and then a field of fire. The Japanese does exactly that. Whenever one of the sniper trees is at the end of a little lane or clear strip in the jungle, loo.. out. The turn of a trail, or the turn of a dry stream bed are ideal spots for snipers.

The Japanese have two favorite maneuvers. The first is an envelopment over "Impassable" terrain by which he hopes to force the opposition to withdraw because of threats on one or both flanks. Little actual fighting is anticipated. Their actual attack is usually made on a very narrow front, and, as a consequence, in great depth; this makes them particularly vulnerable to artillery fire.

Their second favorite maneuver is what has been called a "filleting" attack. It is like filleting a fish — removing the backbone so that the rest can be cut into convenient pieces. In this type of attack, they rush down an arterial supply route with tanks, followed by a dense mass of infantry, on the assumption that, by holding the road and denying us the use of it, we will be forced to withdraw. If they gain this end without fighting, they are highly successful, but if they have to fight they are at a decided disadvantage — not only are they highly vulnerable to artillery fire (the dense-mass of infantry, in depth, with no maneuver space) but, if our troops are up to it, the Japs are vulnerable to a single or double envelopment.

All Japanese operations indicate the tendency to follow a set doctrine without the ability to readjust for changing circumstances. Despite a failure which involved terrific losses, they have repeated the same operation over and over again without attempting to figure out something new.

The Japanese bayonet assaults have been reported as a terrifying attack — but all our units on Guadalcanal loved them. The Jap practice of singing his Banzai song for about 5 minutes prior to his assault has simply been a signal for our troops to load a fresh belt of ammunition in the machine guns, put new clips in rifles and BAR's and to call for the tommy gunners to get in position.

———— ————

In their attack on prepared positions the Japanese have used a more or less standard procedure. Prior to the attack they make every effort, by reconnaissance and ruses, to determine our strength and location and a "soft spot".

After the Japanese have selected their point of attack, they persist in attacking this point in an effort to break through. Should these efforts fail, they sometimes shift to another point but usually return to their original point of attack. Thus, as experience along the Kokoda Trail (New Guinea) indicates, we should not appreciably weaken our defense in the sector originally attacked in order to aid in the defense of some point subsequently attacked.

———— ————

In the Japanese attacks along the Kokoda Trail, the following points were noted:

During their attacks it was not uncommon for the Japanese to replace their forward troops with fresh forces, a few at a time. This was done efficiently and without confusion.

When the Japanese were held up, they immediately dug in for protection. There were slit trenches and foxholes all along their line of retreat on the Kokoda Trail.

b. At Night.

The Japanese selected night-attack objectives by observing our dispositions at sunset. If they failed to find these objectives where they expected them to be, they became confused in the dark because they did not know where to look for us. It would take the Japs about an hour or two to reorganize - this interval was the best time to attack them.

In their night attacks, the Japanese sent advance parties through the dense cover of valleys; they reserved the more open terrain of the higher ground for the main body to approach and make the main effort. To cover up the noises by the advance parties, the main body purposely made noises as it approached.

Frequently the advance parties cleared away jungle growth on terrain over which large units were to approach, spreading luminous paint along the "blazed" trail as a guide.

4. Defense:

a. Enemy Tenacity.

It would be impossible to overstress the tenacity with which the Japanese clung to their prepared positions (in the Buna area). Ordinary grenades, gun and mortar fire were completely ineffective. There were many instances where dugouts were grenaded inside, covered with gasoline and burned, and then sealed with dirt and sand, only to yield - two or three days later - Japanese, who came out fighting. One souvenir hunter, entering a dugout that had been sealed for 4 days, was chased out by a Japanese officer armed with a sword.

------- -------

b. Enemy Positions.

The enemy bunkers and dugouts were constructed of coconut palm logs, dirt, sand and sand bags, covered with natural camouflage. In some instances, pieces of armor plate were set up. The log-and-dirt bunker construction was done carefully and strongly. The corner posts were firmly embedded in the ground and the horizontal logs neatly and strongly attached and interwoven. Several alternate layers of logs and earth were generally used, to give full protection against mortars and light artillery. Roofs were thick; they were made of alternative layers which gave excellent protection. No concrete positions were found.

The bunkers were connected to systems of fire and communication trenches radiating on both sides. In some instances, underground trenches were constructed. These were used by snipers to infiltrate into our midst, even after the enemy units had long been driven from the general ground. Leaves and grass were well used to camouflage all bunkers. The bunkers had been planned and built for just this purpose long before the campaign actually started and the naturally quick jungle growth, sprouting up over the earthworks, gave first class natural camouflage.

The enemy dugout positions were well sited and mutually supporting. It was extremely difficult, if not impossible, to bypass any of the positions each of which had to be reduced in turn.

c. Enemy Tactics.

The Japanese is good at organizing ground with automatic weapons and usually covers approaches into his position by well placed, mutually supporting fires. They usually hold their fire when the first targets appear - they wait for bigger game. They have allowed platoons, or even companies to infiltrate past their positions - so they could cut them off from the rear. It must be recognized, however, that the Jap will seldom leave his position, even when completely outflanked and that he must be reached and killed. However, in spite of his cleverness at concealment and covering avenues of approach he seldom, if ever, traverses or searches with his machine gun and therein lies the key to his destruction. He is also prone to organize ravines and reverse slopes in direct contrast to our practice of occupying the military crest of ridge lines.

Imbued with the offensive idea, the Japanese naturally attempts frequent counterattacks, probably based upon some form of mobile reserve. "On one occasion wrote an Australian officer, "When our attack drove the Jap out, he appeared to become panicky, running from side to side and firing wildly with everything he had; however, a short time later our troops were forced to withdraw by the weight of a counterattack, made by a mobile force in reserve.".

An Australian account of Japanese defensive operations in the Owen Stanley Mountains of New Guinea says:

"The action fought between Myola and Templeton's Crossing was along a narrow ridge on the crest of which runs the main track. The whole length of the ridge is covered by dense jungle, which in some parts consist mostly of bamboo.

When first contacted, the enemy withdrew up a ridge on which he had prepared defensive positions. All approaches to the positions were covered by fire and well camouflaged. Circular, one-man pits were used by each individual soldier. These pits were 2 to 3 feet across and afforded good protection especially from grenades.

It appears that the Japanese keeps his head-down and fires burst after burst from his machine gun blindly spraying the area in front and below his position to create a lot of noise in an attempt to intimidate the attacker.

Machine-gun posts covering the main track were cunningly chosen for position and field of fire. Natural camouflage, such as the butt of a large rotting tree with flanged roots or a small natural ridge beside the track were used to advantage. The positions were well sited for all-around protection.

The Japanese used medium and light machine guns as their main defense; a few riflemen moved to points of vantage as our troops went forward. Hand and discharger grenades were used extensively.

The Japanese likes to move his light machine gun or medium machine gun from place to place during the day. One of our officers, after a reconnaissance, was quite certain that there was no automatic weapon in one position but when we attacked shortly afterwards, a machine gun opened up at the first indication of movement by our troops.

d. On Makin Island.

In their raid on Makin Island, U.S. Marine troops encountered a force of about 90 Japanese soldiers plus about 100 Japanese civilians.

The Japanese set-up consisted of two main positions, a number of lookout points and a mobile reserve which moved on bicycles and in a truck.

One of the main positions was along the edge of the beach on the south side. It consisted of a shallow trench with barbed-wire obstacles to the front.

The other main defense position extended across the island, facing the east. It included a fire trench, 2½ feet wide and 2½ feet deep with the soil thrown up in front. Along the trench, at intervals across the island, were four machine-gun nests. About 75 yards east of the trench a barbed wire fence extended across the island. To block the lone road cutting the defense line, the Japanese used portable barbed-wire "hedgehog" obstacles.

The machine guns and snipers provided the major difficulties for the marines. The marines flattened themselves on the ground when the machine guns opened up but they still were exposed to snipers who had cleverly camouflaged themselves under the fronds of palm trees off to the flanks of the machine guns. The snipers were dressed in a jungle green uniform; some used individual camouflage nets while others hung coconuts all over their body. They were almost impossible to see until they moved or the fronds were shot away. One sniper had the tops of two trees tied together and when spotted he cut the trees loose making it hard to decide which tree he was in.

These snipers tried to pick out troop leaders and radio men.

The marines took care of the snipers first and then knocked out the machine-gun nests. The guns were well sited as to fields of fire and were well concealed.

- 7 -

5. <u>Dummy Snipers</u> (New Guinea).

A patrol advancing up the coast was fired on by a tall tree-top sniper. They halted, located him and apparently shot him down. They then advanced and were fired on again. This happened several times. Thorough investigation revealed that one sniper had been holding up the patrol and dummies had been placed in other trees. These are dropped by a pulley arrangement after the Americans had fired a number of shots. This made them imagine that they had cleared the opposition.

In another case, the sniper's dummy was rigged so that it could be pulled back up into place. The sniper made the mistake of pulling it back up too soon giving away his ruse. The sniper, incidentally, showed very poor marksmanship.

6. <u>Ruses</u>:

The Japanese have used the following ruses in the New Guinea fighting:

a. They dragged a dead United Nations soldier close to our lines and propped him up, expecting that a group of our troops would be sent out to "rescue" him.

b. With the same purpose they placed captured weapons in front of our forces.

c. They fired captured weapons to give the impression that our troops were at the places where the weapons were sited.

d. Over their hats they wore cut-out circular boards to imitate Australian hats.

e. They scattered cast-off garments and equipment on a trail to give the impression they had fled in disorder - actually it was an attempt to ambush our forces.

f. They shook bushes and talked loudly in an attempt to draw our fire.

7. <u>Supply on Guadalcanal</u>.

The serious supply difficulties which confronted the Japanese on Guadalcanal were brought about, to a large degree, by poor distribution and planning. On the same days, we continually encountered Japanese soldiers who were "round-faced and well fed" and those who were emaciated and starving.

This situation was believed to have been due to Japanese overoptimism regarding the outcome of planned attacks. This optimism was transmitted to supply echelons; the Japs had to win a victory on schedule so that their supply operations would continue functioning adequately. One unit had attacked Henderson Field, September 12, 1942, carrying only three day's ration, with no reserve in the rear. Consequently the few who survived the attack were immediately faced with a food shortage.

The Japanese adopted the system of having each company send carriers back for rations which were then carried forward. Because of the rough terrain and our air operations this round trip took as long as 2 or 3 days. These efforts did not provide a full ration for the units so the men were put on reduced rations. This, plus the strain of jungle operations, made the soldiers easy marks for malaria, beri beri and diarrhea. Eventually the condition became so bad in some units that half-sick men were sent to carry rations and the journey took a correspondingly longer time.

Air transportation of food to these troops was attempted with limited success. Late in January, 25 parachutes of food and supplies were dropped to units in the jungle. The parachutes were strafed by our planes, starting some fires, so it is believed only part of the supplies were received by the troops.

The Japanese used all available types of native foods. Ant nests were reported as very good eating by one Japanese soldier. Their forces in New Guinea turned to horse meat when food supplies became low. The meat was processed and issued under the direction of a high echelon.

Although all varieties of food were used by the enemy on Guadalcanal, the normal issue was field rations and dehydrated foods including powdered eggs. It is doubtful if perishable food was issued to front-line troops but some was obtained. In some cases food was buried in the field cemeteries for safekeeping.

Stealing of food became quite common. Ration dumps required extra guards and special precautions. Towards the end, the situation became so bad that an emergency court martial was appointed to deal with the special cases of stealing rations and this court had instructions from the appointing officer to inflict drastic punishment. Rations were reported as being frequently stolen from carriers en route to the front.

JAPANESE PSYCHOLOGY

I RACIAL SOURCES   B*

These extracts are taken from treatises prepared by officers of long residence in Japan — Major S. F. Moran, USMC and Colonel K. F. Baldwin, GSC. (* Throughout the body of this text, extracts from Major Moran's treatise are prefaced by M; those from Colonel Baldwin's by B).

Racially the Japanese are a conglomerate mixture of at least a half dozen types. The original inhabitants of Japan are known as "Ainu". They were a short, stocky people, similar to the Eskimos found farther north. There are still some 20,000 living in the North Japanese Island. It is probable also that in the earlier days there were Negritoes living in the southern part of Japan.

The principal migratory invasions of Japan came from the south and from the west. From the south came a strong influx of Malayan stock with which there was mingled some Negrito blood. There were also invasions by Polynesian peoples from the south and central pacific. From the west at a

very early day, there came a movement of people from the Mongolian Plateau of
Central Asia. In the 6th and 7th centuries there was a heavy influx of
Chinese. In one census taken at that time, one-seventh of the population
consisted of alien Chinese. From time to time a considerable number of
Koreans have entered Japan. Some of these were brought in as prisoners of
war and others just naturally drifted to the Japanese Islands. To these
racial sources could be added a trace of Semitic and Caucasian, but probably
one-half of the Japanese blood is of Malay-Polynesian origin in which the
Malay strain very largely predominates. Most of the other half of the
blood is of Asiatic origin. The result is that characteristics of all these
races and peoples can be found in the Japanese of today but the blending
has been going on for thousands of years.

In 1920 an extensive study was made comparing the measurements
of our first 1,000,000 conscripts in the World War with several classes of
Japanese conscripts for the same period. This study showed that the average
Japanese was twenty pounds lighter and five inches shorter than the average
American soldier. It is very interesting to note that measurements of the
Japanese prisoners captured on Bataan showed that the Japanese average nine-
teen pounds lighter and five inches shorter than the average American. The
Japanese, being a small man physically, has many of the reactions which are
common to small people generally. He looks upon larger people as bullies.
Japanese jujitsu is a system of physical training by which a smaller man
can conquer a larger one by means of tricks, surprises and catching the man
off balance. This idea of fighting an opponent prevails throughout Japan,
even to the heads of the army and navy themselves so that anyone dealing
with Japanese must expect them to employ surprise and trickery in doing the
things least expected and to do what is often the most difficult in order
to affect surprise.

II. GEOGRAPHY & CLIMATE AND ITS EFFECT UPON THE JAPANESE M

The Japanese have been unquestionably a very brave people from
primitive times but at the same time their geographical isolation has given
them a remarkable protection from foreign enemies. They are inclined to
attribute the fact of their never having been overrun or conquered to their
supreme innate valor. For example, it is unquestionable that, at the time
of the attempted Mongol invasion of Japan in the XIII century, the Japanese
fought as valiantly and fiercely as any people in history, and, in some
respects, with a great inferiority of tactical skill and of equipment.
But the defeat of the Mongol hords was at the same time due, to no incon-
siderable extent, to a violent storm off the Japanese coast (memories of the
Spanish Armada come to mind) that ultimately scattered the invading fleet;
also the impracticable nature of landing large bodies of men owing to
unwieldiness and the fact that the invading hords were only half-hearted
in their desire to accomplish their objectives. But according to the popular
conception of the Japanese, their valor per se was what won the victory.
A tradition has been built up in the minds of the people.

To sum up: Japan, the country and the Japanese people themselves
are inseparably connected in the minds of the nation. When there is added
to that the fact that the Japanese are largely excluded, through immigration
restrictions from other countries, it will be seen that they are thus thrown

back upon themselves and their own country in a way that stimulates still more what we may call their "rock and rill" patriotism. And when added to this we have the Emperior-tradition people in a closely knit nation whose morale will not easily disintegrate.

III. FUNDAMENTAL INFLUENCES   B

For hundreds of years and in some instances for thousands of years, the Japanese have been living under influences which have been extremely important in moulding the whole character of their thought and action. These are often not readily understood by outsiders but in the making of the Japanese they have been and continue to be very vital.

a. <u>Japan is a land of ancient tradition.</u> Not only does the imperial line represent to the Japanese some 2600 years of time but the very countryside itself speaks in an ancient language. There are temples and little shrines on every hill and in every corner in most of Japan. There are old Buddhas which have been there for 1200 years or longer. Every village or place is characterized by some folk-lore legend concerned with its heroesor with its historical past. Machiman Taro who returned to his homeside after being 185 years at the Dragon Palace is the Japanese counterpart of our Rip Van Winkle. The monuments showing where he lived and tales relating his story are told with apparent authenticity by the people of his village. The graves of the 47 Ronin in Tokyo at which incense is kept constantly burning, although only about 300 years old speak of the past. In the little shrine by the wayside dwells the spirit of some ancestor who lived on this earth 500 to 800 years ago. The people of the village greatly revere this little shrine and entertain the spirit once or twice a year with playful ceremonies. The children, as they grew up, are taught these legends and stories by their mothers and their nurses. They are bound to believe many of them though they may be purely traditional fiction. Even white children raised in this atmosphere are influenced by this indoctrination. I know of several individual cases. Since from the earilest days the Japanese have worshiped their ancestors it is natural that they are very attentive to anything which goes back in the past to their fathers.

b. <u>The influence of Chinese culture and language.</u> In the sixth and seventh centuries large numbers of educated Chinese came to Japan. With them they brought the Chinese philosophy and the Chinese literature. The doctrines of Confucius and the teachings of Buddha spread rapidly in Japan and the Japanese for his classical reading today turns to the books of Mencius and Confucius. For a time it looked as if Japan would become a Buddhist nation. Even the members of the imperial household were equally influenced by Buddhist teachings. Buddhism in its own clever way accepted the gods of the early Shinto and explained that they had merely been reincarnated in Japan. The Japanese to this day are really Shintofied-Buddhists. Pure Shintoists in Japan are rare.

Prior to the coming of the Chinese the Japanese had no literature. They adopted the Chinese characters. These, together with a short syllabic alphabet, constitute the characters which make up the Japanese writing today. Actually, in modern life it is a great handicap, for it requires two years longer for a Japanese to complete a college education that it would if the same instruction had been given from the first in English.

c. The influence of Feudalism. Society was divided into various strata. The Emperor and imperial household were very much in the background. The chief feudal leader might marry his daughter and receive his blessings but the common people knew very little about the existance of such a man as Emperor. The feudal leaders were in a class by themselves. Surrounding them were their retainers known as Samurai who were warriors wearing two swords and chain armor and they in turn were guided by the strictest kind of regulations. They were always looked up to as being the corps d'elite and when they walked the streets they could practically do as they pleased to the lower classes of society. To kill a member of the outcast class of Eta was not a crime at all, and, in fact, very little thought was given to the rights of the other lower groups. Our earliest visitors to Japan spoke of the strutting and pompous attitude of the Samurai and yet they are the god worshipped idols of the Japanese soldier of today.

d. Japan is a land of limited areas and small things. Not only are the people small but the farmed area is small; the houses are small, the gardens very small. You are in surroundings which show life in minature. Four or five people must live off the production of every acre of ground farmed because only about one-sixth of all the land is arable. This limitation of resources and smallness of things has developed in the Japanese a sense of careful utilization of everything they possess. There is almost no waste. The people have developed along lines of cleanliness and neatness as is evident in their homes and gardens. There is rarely a big show of things in Japan. One would think that these influences would develop a people with extremely narrow vision and undoubtedly that is the tendency. The Japanese being closely knit in family circles, the love for the little home and the obligation to the family is deep all along the line. The individual has been submerged in the family.

e. The influences of misfortune and disasters. Japan is a land where tragedy stalks. There are earthquakes every day; there are disasterous earthquakes every year. There are volcanos in active eruption and every year there are very disasterous floods which sweep into the low lying cities and destroy thousands of lives. Until recent years, fires were extremely common and the old saying in Tokyo was "a fire every seven years". Tokyo has three times been destroyed by earthquakes; the earthquake of December 1, 1933 killed more than 100,000 people and inflicted a financial loss on Japan relatively as high as the whole First World War burden on the United States. It was terrific. It may have helped to postpone the present war and, I might add, now would be a good time for another earthquake.

We get something of the Japanese reaction to such calamities by studying what happened at the time of this great earthquake. We see the contrast in Japanese psychology. Someone spread the rumor that Koreans and Chinese were poisoning wells and starting fires and immediately mobs of Japanese attacked Chinese, Koreans and, in some cases, their own people without reason. Between two thousand and three thousand people were actually murdered at that time.

Everyone literally went crazy and this may be the pattern which will be followed by the Japanese in case of violent bombing and destruction of their great cities. I would hate to be a prisoner of war located near a large Japanese city which was bombed.

Life has been so grim and so difficult for most of the Japanese that the tribulations of war are much less burdensome to him than to us. The farmer boy who has worked slavishly in the mud for his rice crop, receiving little or no profit, living on poor food and seeing storms and misfortunes take their toll, is the background of the Japanese fighting army and he is accustomed to hardship and misfortune.

f. I would mention as a 6th influence that impact of modern civilization came as a great shock to the Japanese people.

Commodore Perry came to Japan in the 50's and broke the latch to the door. Japanese missions hastened abroad to find a world that had been taken over very largely by European countries with little left for Japan in case she wished to become a nation. However, within 20 years after Perry's visit, great changes did take place. Feudalism was abolished; the boy Emperor was brought from seclusion and placed on the throne in 1867. He was the great Emperor Meiji. By his early edicts he sent his leaders abroad to study governments and politics and constitutions but they also studied industrial and military development.

In 1871 the Samurai, as such, ceased to be soldiers of the feudal lords and a conscript army was formed by the central government. A few years later it fought and won a very difficult war with disgruntled Samurai. Missionaries and teachers poured into Japan. In the 70's and 80's for a time it looked as if Japan might become a modernized Christian state.

The population started to grow and with the coming of sanitation and removal of feudal restrictions, it has increased until now there are about 75 million Japanese. Their leaders early saw that they must have more territory, more room and now they want a population of 100,000,000.

In the 70's they extended their sovereignty to include the Bonin Islands, the Liushu Islands and the Kuriles. But they had eyes upon continental Asia. By 1894 they were able to successfully challenge China. This gave them the island of Formosa, which has been developed into a wonderful garden spot for Japan. They were forced out of Manchuria by the influence of Germany, Russia and France. They took on Russia in 1904, absorbed Russia's control of Manchuria and secured the south half of Sakhalin Island. In 1910, in an unscrupulous manner, they grabbed Korea and annexed it bodily. During the World War, they were nominally aligned with the Allies but at the same time perpetrated their nefarious twenty-one demands upon China. Together with us, they occupied Eastern Siberia which we forced them to give back to the Russians at the Washington Conference in 1922. They extended their power and hold in Manchuria and set up a puppet state known as Manchukuo. They tried by all manner of intrigue and threat to secure full control in China.

Everywhere they have gone they have met countries already populated or fairly so. Their method has been to destroy the educated and leading class, set up a puppet institution to which they could dictate, develop the country for their benefit and to a much lesser extent, for the benefit of the native population. They have not moved to any of these outside lands in great numbers. They are the corporals, the captains and the generals in developing these regions. Nowhere have they won the love and esteem of the people because they seem to fail utterly to understand the people of other countries. They frequently use our Monroe Doctrine and our occupation of troubled Latin American countries as a precedent and excuse for more drastic action in the Asiatic theater. Certainly for the last 50 years some of the Japanese leaders have had world-wide ambitions and the military group in authority definitely set as its goal the occupation of all Eastern Asia and the Dutch East Indies to be accomplished within this generation.

"The Imperial Influence". With the abolishment of feudalism - the imperial position became greatly changed. There was a return to the early ideology of Japan and a going back into the past for the things justifying the imperial system. Education was extended to include much instruction on the Emperor and the Imperial line. He became the inspiration of all the Japanese people. The loyalty formerly shown to the feudal lords was diverted to the imperial family but the early leaders as they developed began to use the imperial sanction for fostering their own advancement. Much literature appeared showing "the Way of the Gods" and how the national spirit should be centered in the Emperor. His relationship is one of co-brotherhood; he performs certain rights and ceremonies but to the average Japanese he is his link to Heaven.

While religious freedom was guaranteed, the priests and temples came under rigorous control. It was fairly easy to establish an educational system which developed patriotism and loyalty to the Emperor. These ideas are very deep in the life of nearly every Japanese. No one in Japan would think of harming the Emperor or causing him pain or worry. He is above even an evil thought.

There are two things in Japan that are never mentioned with criticism - one is the Emperor and the other the army. The Japanese simply do not speak critically on these subjects. If the army does something which is inexcusable he does not believe it; he has been too deeply taught and indoctrinated.

IV. THE EMPEROR M

The Japanese nation is an Emperor-centered nation. In certain respects this can hardly be over-emphasized. It is an historical fact, not open to question, that the imperial line of Japan extends back in unbroken succession further, much further that the royal line of any other country. The Japanese propagandists are never tired of pointing out this feature of their political set-up.

With the coming to the throne of the Emperor Meiji in 1868 the modern era in Japan really begins. He had around him many able advisers determined to make Japan a modern nation and a strong nation. The Shogunate had passed out and Tokyo became the capital of modern Japan, both the political capital and the court capital. The point of immediate concern to us here is that these advisers around the Emperor, these makers of the modern political structure of Japan, took this hoary Emperor-tradition and remade it. They did not modernize it; just the reverse. They buttressed the germs of historical truth regarding this Emperor-tradition with features made up out of whole cloth as it were. They built up a myth. Two features may be especially pointed out here:

a. The date 660 B.C. was arbitrarily set as the date of the beginning of the reign of the "first Emperor", the reign of an Emperor receiving his charter of power, as it were, from the Sun Goddess, his ancestor. It should be noted at this point that the holy Emperor of Japan is not crowned by some one; he does not have a coronation in the Western meaning of the word. He himself assumes the throne, i.e., he ascends to the throne in his own inate and holy right, the theory being that he is not dependent upon anyone else for this position and honor. Though there is no shadow of historical evidence to indicate that there was an Emperor anywhere nearly so long ago as this, yet this date, 660 B.C., or to be explicit, February 11, 660 B.C., is set as the official date of the start of the Japanese empire, and February 11 each year is a national holiday (Kigensetsu) of peculiar significance to the Japanese. This date is taught to the children of primary schools in Japan as an historical fact.

b. The Emperor granted a constitution to his subjects limiting his own powers. But the point to note is that the philosophy of government contained in this act is that it was the Emperor himself, spontaneously and owing to his own benign nature, who graciously deigned to give his grateful and awestruck subjects a constitution. In fact, this point of view runs through all the orthodox political philosophy of Japan. That is to say, here is no analogy with the English Magna Carta which the powerful English barons forced King John to give them as their right. Such a conception would be unthinkable in Japan so far as their own Emperor is concerned. To put it another way, the individual Japanese unlike the individual American, is not a citizen of his country but a subject. It is true the British also use the word "subject" in distinction to the American word "citizen" but there is no distinction here in fact. It is simply a hangover from ancient times in the use of the word.

The question with which we are concerned, to put it in vulgar parlance, is: How seriously do the Japanese take this Emperor-business? Do they "fall for" all this? Foreigners often ask, in wonder, "Do the Japanese really believe so and so?"

The answer to this question should be divided into two parts: (1) the attitude of the twentieth century Japanese prior to, say, 1931 the year Japan grabbed Manchuria; and (2) since 1931, that is, the past decade when Japan has been embarked on a campaign to treaty breaking and international gangsterism all smeared over with pious phrases and high sounding slogans.

(1) Before 1931 the simply country folk took the Emperor myth more or less at its face value. There was no particular reason to question it; there was no immediate crisis confronting the nation to make the belief

or disbelief in the complete myth of vital importance. But certainly very
few educated people took it at its face value, excepting always, a few fanatics.
The government, the police, the military did not care especially what theory
of the Emperor was taught in the universities, even in the law department,
so long as it was confined to academic school room discussion and not proclaimed from the house tops to the common people. As for the primary schools
the orthodox Emperor-myth was presented as a matter of course. But in spite
of all this sacred Emperor-tradition and the alleged invariably undying devotion
to their supreme lord on the part of the Japanese through the centuries,
every well-educated and informed Japanese knew that some of their Emperors
of the past had been libertines, some just plain incompetents, some had been
assassinated by those giving lip service, some forced to abdicate and a more
amenable puppet placed on the throne; and in at least one case, upon the death
of the Emperor, he had lain for days in Kyoto, unburied because no money was
provided for his burial. It was also no secret that the Emperor Taisho, the
father of the present Emperor and the son of the great Emperor Meiji was a
weakling in body and in mind; and underground reports even said that on one
occasion he had done rather childish and absurd things while addressing the
diet formally at its regular annual opening while his loyal subjects of the
legislature stood with bowed heads at still attention, technically in solemn
and awed silence at his august presence. And when it was eventually announced
that the then Crown Prince (now the present Emperor) had been declared Regent
owing to his Majesty's "poor health", those "in the know" realized that the
poor Emperor was "all washed up" and simply couldn't make the grade. He
passed out of the picture and died shortly afterwards.

(2)   Since 1931 a change has become apparent to the most casual
observer. Even before 1931 at the signing of the naval treaty in London, with
Great Britain, the United States and Japan participating and the 5-5-3 ratio was
agreed upon, it will be remembered that the official Japanese delegate, in
conformity with the others, signed "in the name of the people of Japan".
A furor was caused in Japan by the purists and the super-nationalists who
declared that only the Emperor himself could speak for his people.

After the grabbing (I use the word advisedly) of Manchuria by
Japan in 1931, and the eyes of the world were focussed upon this defiance of
international law, the Japanese militarists and super-nationalists began to
take stock. They needed to justify their recent actions and their future
plans. And they saw that they must stiffen the people and harden them. The
militarists had been longing to "get tough" for a number of years. But they
had been a growing liberalism in Japan. At one popular election for representatives for the Diet the astounding result was proclaimed that 15 socialist
seats had been won! This truly was a remarkable advance in liberalism for
Japan. The police, backed by the Home Department of the Japanese government,
began to talk continually of "kiken shiso" (dangerous thoughts) and continually
cautioned that devoted subjects must be on guard against such ideas. Arrests
for the alleged holding of "dangerous thoughts" were common. The military,
in its turn, repeatedly hinted darkly that the nation must be ready for an
emergency (hijoji). This word, in fact, was used so often that it became
almost a by-word to play with. As the days, months and even years went by,
and no real "emergency" arose, even legislators were reported indignantly
to have inquired, "what is this 'emergency' we are continually being told to
be ready for? No emergency seems to be emerging!"

But now things began to tighten up. By the time of the start of the war with China (dubbed by the Japanese Government "the China incident") in July 1937, the people were prepared more or less for rigorous conditioning by the authorities.

V. THE JAPANESE SOLDIER M

The question whether the Japanese think of themselves as a super race is one which much nonsense is sometimes written by western writers. It is in regard to this question particularly that we must be careful to have in mind whom we mean and to what classes in Japan we refer when we talk glibly about "the Japanese".

In military prowess, in patriotism, in bravery, in fortitude most Japanese do think of themselves as more or less in a class apart from the rest of mankind -- that is, superior. But the above-mentioned qualities are only a part of the general characteristics and features of any race and I believe that most sane Japanese recognize this fact.

What of the Japanese soldier and the indoctrination that goes to make up his morale? And what of the people's attitude toward him and toward super-nationalism?

The Japanese army is democratic. Any man who has the desire, ability and physical qualifications may devote his life to the armed services and be educated to be an officer. There is thus no snobbery in the Japanese army based on social position. The only distinctions there are, are those between the different grades of officers and enlisted men. Here, in some respects, there is a stiffness and fine distinction over-exaggerated from our standpoint. It is well known that the lot of the Japanese private has been made easier than it was a few decades ago; that is, his treatment being made more humane, if that is the word to use, while at the same time not relaxing rigid discipline in the slightest.

This above-mentioned democratic structure of the Japanese army is natural when one realizes that Japan has and always has had since it became a modern nation, universal conscription. As a result, soldiers are a most common sight in Japan, even in peace time. No special respect or deference is paid to them by the general public, for all male subjects serve in the forces sooner or later unless physically disqualified.

All Japanese soldiers can read, thanks to the instituting of compulsory primary school education in the Meiji era. It was thought not so many years ago that a nation that could read could not be fooled; the people of such a nation, so the theory went, could form their own independent judgments. But we know now in this age of rigid censorship and at the same time clever, systematic propaganda in newspaper, magazine and book, we can control the thoughts of those who can read even better than we could control the thoughts of the illiterates. So the thoughts and point of view of the Japanese soldiers is largely a product of carefully controlled propaganda and censorship. Or to put it in another way, he is continually bathed in an atmosphere of a certain predetermined type.

The backbone of the Japanese army is the simple country boy. His life was meager and rigorous even before coming into the army. It was not only awfully simple but more or less simply awful! So induction into the army for him was no nightmare of strenuous physical activity and simple spartan fare. His body was far huskier than the city boy. He knew what it was to work to suffer and even then hardly to make a living. He was used to being a mere cog in the Japanese family system; he was used to the orthodox type of family regimentation. So the transition to army life and army standards, to army ideals and army discipline and withal to army indoctrination was not so great a change as might be supposed. And in addition to all this, it was emphasized in season and out of season that he was the Emperor's soldier, - in fact, in the last analysis, the personal representative and protector of the Emperor. Thus, theoretically he is the model of perfection the model of discipline. This is the tradition the ordinary Japanese accepts: His Emperor's army is composed entirely of vigorously trained men, pure of motive, simple and frugal in tastes and ready to die at the drop of a hat for their beloved and august Emperor. Here again, it is this belief on the part of the people regarding their army that made it impossible for many Japanese to believe that their troops would do anything dastardly, anything irregular, anything counter to their supposedly never-relaxed discipline.

> (A Japanese, highly educated, partially in America, was told of the far from uncommon practice in Shanghai and environs, in the past few years of Japanese officers, for their own personal profit, selling army gasoline to Chinese and to other foreigners. Irrefutable evidence was offered. But this Japanese not only would not but could not bring himself to believe this of the Emperor's troops. "If true, it must have been done for the benefit of the army's exchequer and not for personal gain." And he added significantly, "Such a thing might happen in other armies but not in the Japanese Army.")

As has already been pointed out, it is only since 1931 and the seizing of Manchuria, that rabid nationalism has been made a fetish of by the Japanese military controlled government. Before that time the army and its ideals and desires were not causing the people in general much concern. Avoiding conscription, through amateur attempts to ruin the eyesight and the like were reported in newspapers now and then. Few really wanted to join the army. If they were caught there was no help for it and their friends and acquaintances all went through the formality of exclaiming "Omedetō" (congratulations) and of seeing them off at the station when they departed for their training (nyūei) as raw recruits.

But at all times, the Japanese implicitly accepts the assumption that the Japanese army is invincible and that the Japanese soldier would never surrender. For is not the soldier and the entire army, the guardian of the Emperor? For the Japanese soldier to surrender would be an insult to the Emperor, so the theory is. Even to retreat or to make general tentative plans for retreat (except possibly for a brief period for strategic reasons and then only better to advance again) is abhorrent to Japanese strategy. Their whole war program is geared to attack. They are trained literally to "do or die". There is something theatrical about all this; this thinking that in the last analysis even if equipment and numbers are inadequate the Japanese spirit (Nippon Seishin) that we are continually having dinned in our ears will be the deciding factor and bring triumph to the Emperor's army. But at the same time, we must realize that the Japanese soldier is a decidedly tough specimen, well conditioned and well trained. We know that Japanese have surrendered, - at least been surrounded and captured. There have been reports for the last four years of Japanese prisoners in China; General MacArthur, while still in the Philippines, reported having some Japanese prisoners. One of the first questions asked by the Japanese general, Yamashita, of the British commanding general at the time of the surrender of Singapore was, "Have you any Japanese prisoners?" As for retreating, cases have been actually witnessed in China of a Japanese bombing plane, suddenly confronted by a superior force, dropped all its bombs into the river below to lighten its load and fleeing for safety.

In the presentation of war to the Japanese public, all its horrors are completely ignored. Photographs either in magazines, newspapers or the movies showing ghastly scenes are strictly prohibited. That is why war propaganda movies and war news reels in Japan are so tame. Soldiers are shown marching, soldiers are shown charging with bayonet. Who is awaiting that bayonet is not only never pictured but the assumption is never allowed to arise in the spectator's mind that on the other side there may also be a soldier likewise with a bayonet equally brave and equally well trained. No, it is always the heroic Japanese soldier, invincible, charging some (imaginary) dastardly enemy of his Emperor such as the despised Chinese who has not good sense enough and fairness or mind enough to appreciate the enlightening paternalism of the Japanese! In news-reels depicting the war in China, about the only things shown were troops marching along roads in China, troops crossing rivers in China, and, most common of all, soldiers standing on the high wall of some Chinese city, presumably just captured, waving a Japanese flag, holding up their hands and shouting "Banzai" ("Hurrah!") That the Chinese must have thought of this continual waving of Japanese flags almost in their faces, as it were, does not seem to be a problem to be concerned about from the Japanese viewpoint.

Furthermore, the Japanese are not allowed to see seriously wounded soldiers in the hospitals. Hospitals where the army wounded are kept are very difficult to get into, even for relatives and friends. But every now and then officially O.K'd pictures of convalescent wounded are shown in the newspapers, - these wounded shown smiling happily, even gleefully, according to the caption, with the thought presumably dominant in their minds of having been of service to their Emperor. I have even seen pictures in the Japanese newspapers and magazines showing soldiers totally blinded from combat action, sitting up in bed with admiring nurses and other convalescents around them, depicted as smiling brightly at the thought that they are valiant servants of the Emperor only too proud to do their bit.

And now let us take up the "shot in the arm", the hypodermics, innumerable and varied that the Japanese people received in the decade beginning with 1931 to make them more alert to the appeals of the hell-bent military.

By hell-bent military, it is not meant literally the whole Japanese army and navy system. It is meant that:

(a) Certain higher officers, professional fire-eaters, such as Admiral Suetsugu and General Araki, to mention just two; holding high motives, according to their limited light, and thinking of nothing but the national prestige of a Greater Japan and their Emperor's expanding glory.

(b) Groups of younger officers, particularly of the army, itching for action, thinking they could "lick the world", contemptuous of democracy and modern international obligations, whose only code they express with the vague phrase, the "Imperial Way" (Kodo).

(c) Fanatics among the laymen, narrow super-patriots, ranting against any spirit of internationalism, taking the Emperor-myth literally and witch-hunting for any who do not swallow it whole. The Black Dragon Society, with the elderly fanatic, Toyama, in Tokyo is a primary spark plug of this group.

These three groups take their fanaticism even right into the army and navy and war against them, their own fellow-officers and against government officials. They consider many respected army and navy higher-ups as mossbacks, "Kabikusai" (smelling of mold), led astray by Western influences and shibboleths and not alive to the real implications of the 100% "true" Imperial Way.

These three groups would stop at nothing to accomplish their ends even against their government, - even against their own army and navy departments. They are thus actually an unorganized group above the government and above the army and navy, not at all representing what to us would be the saner and fairer elements in army, navy or government.

A few years back one of these rabid younger officers, classified as ("b") above, cut down and killed with his sword one of the very highest officers in the army, the Inspector General of Military Training. This morbid military fanatic gave as his reason (to boil down his rantings into one simple and fairly intelligible phrase) that the Inspector was negligent in his duties in that he did not adequately realize the grievous condition into which the country was sliding and that in these times of emergency and danger to the very fundamental principles of the Imperial Way, such a complacent soul had no right to be holding a position of such importance and responsibility in his Majesty's armed services. And this young officer was not alone in all this; other officers were back of him, heart and soul.

This is the type of officer responsible for the sinking of the Panay in 1937.

VI. COMPARATIVE IDEALS B

The Japanese soldiers have been taught that in war they must be prepared to sacrifice everything. Their doctrines repeatedly stress that "morale is to material as ten is to one" and their training is based very much upon this hypothesis. In forced marches the Japanese soldier was never permitted to fall out unless he became unconscious. In case a man fell out of ranks he was laid on his back and the sergeant stuck the knuckle of a fist into his open eye, if he flinched he was still conscious and he was then kicked back into line and compelled to march until he completed the journey or until he fell unconscious. After long forced marches leaders frequently ordered the men to run on the double around the barracks when they were in sight of the rest. This, they said, was to show the men that they still had fight and strength left in them.

The Japanese in battle is manifestly fanatical. His is the spirit of attack and that can always be expected even though his chances of success are very remote. When driven into close quarters he fights with great desperation, bolstering himself with the spirit and instructions he has had, to die rather than surrender.

Our troops were astounded at the battle conditions in which the Japanese live, with dead lying about for days, or even weeks before they were finally themselves eliminated. This can be at least partially explained. In the first place, when a Japanese recruit joins the army he is told that if he does the things he is instructed to do and observes the health rules and regulations laid down by his officers he will not be sick and if he is, it's his own fault. No doubt much of this doctrine is carried into the field and the soldier is extremely reluctant to report himself as being sick. The medical department too is not anxious to make him a patient unless he is indeed very sick believing that a man should fight on in spite of physical handicaps. The dead lie about unburied as the desire of the Japanese is that all bodies should be cremated and the ashes returned to Japan. Their spirits will be deified in the Yasukuni Shrine in Tokyo and a portion of the ashes sent home to the family. This is certainly one important reason why the Japanese are reluctant to bury their dead. Many of the Japanese were raised on farms where they have worked with the most offensive, foulsmelling fertilizer in the world and puddled this into the muck and mud with their feet. They are accustomed to vile and terrible odors and have just steeled themselves against such surroundings. Some of their senses have become absolutely blunt and do not register. They reach a form of fatalistic determination under terrible conditions which is hard for us to understand.

Judging from captured documents, great stress is still being placed upon morale training and the early heroes of this war are greatly honored, notably the midget submarine commanders who gave their lives at Pearl Harbor. Parents are taught that if their son gives his life in this war, they should consider it an honor above all others and accept this as a special favor of the gods. They are still driving the old morale machine at full speed and continue to get good results from the standpoint of willingness to sacrifice on the part of the Japanese in the field or at home. The points brought out in the above make the Japanese very excellent soldiers especially for ground work infantry and he cannot be defeated by green and untrained troops. He can be wiped out or defeated of course by superior trained troops with superior equipment and superior generalship. The first essential is to strike with surprise and upset the enemy. Never let a Jap take you by surprise for that is just what he desires most to do.

MILITARY METHODS

The military organization in 1925 began systematically to propagandize in all the higher schools and colleges of Japan. The system was borrowed from the American R.O.T.C. It was carried out so completely in Japan that the army got control of the spiritual and cultural training in all of these institutions. It has thereby, for the last twenty years, dictated the doctrines with which the growing Japanese have been imbued so that the younger generation in Japan, in spite of its modern education, is probably more devoted to conquest and expansion than any previous generation. There is a bit of the Nazi method in this process.

It is a peculiarity of the Japanese army that a junior may perform all manner of cruel acts against an enemy or a non-Japanese and his acts will not be punished by his superiors provided that he cloaks himself with patriotic motives. No Japanese general is going to punish a Japanese captain for killing a few prisoners of war or for bayoneting Chinese as a means of instruction or for holding an enemy killing contest among his non-commissioned officers. The files of Washington and London must contain at least 1000 incidents in Korea, Manchuria, Siberia and China of acts which we would call cruel and inhuman and which remain unpunished.

If Japan treats our prisoners of war with consideration it is because she expects to reap some advantage by so doing. In the war with Russia the Russian prisoners of war were well treated and this was used as a means of undermining Russian fighting morale. In this war the desire to impress Philippinos, Malayans, Chinese and others with the superiority of the Japanese over the Occidental seems to be the prevailing idea. In this respect it might be added that the Japanese utterly fail to distinguish one Occidental from another — the German or the Italian is no different from the American and the Britisher.

In Korea in 1919, an American was visiting the palace or pavilion occupied by the former Korean Queen. Shortly after the war with Russia, under the pretext of need of protection, the Japanese had placed a guard at the legation in Seoul. The American questioned the Japanese guide by saying, "This is where the Korean Queen was killed" and the guide replied "Yes, she heard the noise of our men mounting the fence there: she ran to the edge of the pavilion where some soldiers grabbed her by the hair, and here", pointing to the ground, "her head was cut off. It was left in that fountain over there". This murder occurred about 1910.

In 1918 a Japanese Lieutenant was sent to investigate a small Korean village. A Japanese M.P. had been killed twenty miles away but this being a Christian village, the villagers were blamed. After assembling all the inhabitants of the town in the little church, the lieutenant read the Imperial Rescript, barred the door and set the place on fire, thus exterminating the entire population. A Japanese officer was asked what happened to the lieutenant, "Oh", he said, "he may have made a mistake in judgment, but he did this out of a patriotic motive, and, of course, no punishment was administered". When Japan took over Korea, she gave the few Korean loyalists no notice whatever, demanding immediate surrender. Some did not understand and they were simply slaughtered in cold blood. These methods followed in Korea are the same as those wherever the Japanese troops have gone - in Manchuria, in Siberia, in China and now in the Philippine Islands and in the Dutch East Indies. There are hundreds of similar cases.

Back in Japan an American officer had an experience on how not to talk with a Japanese. In 1918 he was inspecting a howitzer at the Yokosuka harbor defenses. He was the only American there among a group of curious Japanese soldiers and officers. At the gun he thoughtlessly asked the corporal at the sight if it was graduated in meters. To his surprise the corporal asked the question of the sergeant, the sergeant of the lieutenant, the lieutenant of the captain, the captain of the major, the major of the colonel and the colonel of the brigadier, thus going in a complete circle around the American officer. The brigadier nodded favorably to the colonel and the nod went back to the corporal who said "Yes". The lesson: Never ask a Japanese any question in the presence of his senior. In fact, better still, never ask a Japanese a question or talk with him intimately unless you do so alone. This is a good thing to bear in mind in the interrogation of prisoners of war.

VII. WILL THE JAPANESE MORALE CRACK IN THIS WAR?

HOW AND UNDER WHAT CONDITIONS?   M

It goes without saying that there can be no positive answer to the second of these two questions until the event itself actually happens, then there will be no need to ask questions. As for the first of these two questions, we can of course assume that no nation's morale is 100% attack proof. And, as has been repeatedly emphasized in this study, the Japanese are human, just like the rest of us, so there is no need to make an exception in their case.

Let up point out some interesting features of the psychology of the present day Japanese:

(1) When the war with China started in 1937 and from then on the radio (which is entirely government controlled, with no advertising sponsors) blared out daily, almost hourly, the necessity for every Japanese to be self-sacrificing, to be patriotic, to fall in line, etc. The newspapers did the same. All this was so incessant, so insistent and persistent that one could not help but wonder. Why the necessity for all this? If the Japanese are even one-third as patriotic as the official apologists would have us believe, why this over-emphasis? There was something suspicious about it all.

(2) Why has Japanese officialdom so persistently kept the use of the short wave radio away from its people? What is it that they fear so much? The writer once pointedly asked this question of a Japanese naval officer who was addressing a picked group of Americans soon after the start of the China-Japan war, a meeting arranged by the authorities to enlighten the Americans as to the "Justice" of Japan's cause. The question was asked at the time of a question period. The naval officer, in answering, was most patently embarrassed and said in a low voice, while hanging his head, that it was to keep dangerous thoughts, such as communistic propaganda, particularly from China and Russia from entering Japan.

"But what of the famous Japanese patriotism we hear so much about? England, America and other countries who bitterly oppose communism in principle still allow their people to have short wave radios. Does it mean that the Japanese government does not trust its own people?" To this the Japanese naval officer made no reply except to mumble in an almost inaudible voice, "I have nothing more to add." (The preceding is practically a verbatim report of the conversation).

The preceding incident makes one wonder exactly how deep, how much to-the-bitter-end is a patriotism whose foundations, whose idealism cannot stand hearing any point of view but the point of view of those in power. What will happen when they do hear other points of view?

(3) Though the Japanese are a patient people and used to being regimented as has been pointed out on more than one occasion in this study, yet they can rise up in furious indignation, - the worm will turn. Such a case was the famous rice riots soon after the close of the last World War. The daily life of the ordinary Japanese is dependent in a peculiar way upon the price of rice. At the period mentioned, the price of this basic food commodity rose to such heights that crowds in different parts of the country took the matter into their own hands, - a case of "direct action". They smashed shops and looted them of rice even defying the police. The patient common people had shown a spirit of rebellion undreamed of. Of course, there were no really political implications in this rebellion, but it certainly gave the authorities a headache. Immediately the government began to appropriate large sums of money for public relief and for starting various forms of public welfare work. The large municipal social settlement in Northern Osaka was built entirely with money from this appropriation, to cite just one concrete result. In fact, modern government social work in Japan on any large scale, may be said to have started with the money appropriated at the time of these rice riots. And ever since the Japanese government has kept its watchful eye on the price of rice.

This makes one wonder, if, at the same time as a real smashing military defeat of Japan (a major naval defeat, or a sustained, devastating major bombing attack, for example), the common people, through deprivation and suffering realize that those who advocated this war are getting them nowhere. Then what?

(4) The Japanese, though intensely patriotic, as has been already pointed out, is no more above bribery and crooked politics than the people of other countries. The navy contract scandal of the early part of this century was notorious. Bribery and municipal corruption, buying of votes and intimidation are most common occurrences. Professional thugs (gorotsuki) are a well-known feature of Japanese life and politics. Even when at the start of the China-Japan war in 1937 the government put into effect drastic economic restrictions, evasion was a daily occurrence and only iron-clad regulations and severe penalties made the system work. Patriotism never yet, in any country, has completely cured among every member of its population the disease known as "itching palm".

With the above in mind, it may thus be said that there are those in Japan who would "cooperate" with the enemy for financial considerations. And when to this is added that among the civilian Japanese outside of Japan such as in the South Seas and in China there are many who are riffraff and the scum of Japanese society, certain possible chinks in the Japanese war armor may be readily surmised. "A word to the wise".

CONCLUSION B

Our immediate concern is to make the war easier for use in battle but to hasten the days of peace we must also undermine the fighting morale of the Japanese people at home. These are difficult tasks. General MacArthur has been sound in not resorting to propaganda and psychological warfare until after we had won victories of importance. The most valuable morale factor is the defeat of army after army of Japanese. The capture of the Philippines or the occupation of strong bases from which aircraft can cover Japan proper will have deep repercussions upon the home front – especially upon the leaders – though these facts may never reach the Japanese troops isolated in China. Tojo and his crowd are responsible for this war. When heavy defeat stares them in the face they will go – probably by suicide – and others will take their places until the next defeat. The crushing of Germany will send a chill throughout Japan that might bring wide political and military readjustments. We must anticipate that Japan may be willing to relinquish part of her gains in order to secure a temporary peace. Japan withdrew from Siberia and Shantung Province after the last war without being driven out by any army. She is unlikely to go back this way again but she might do so. It's another unpredictable. However, we must plan on having to fight all the way back to Japan.

POW INTERROGATION REPORT

1. PREAMBLE

PW is the son of a regular Army officer. His father died at an early age while holding the rank of captain in the Imperial Japanese army. PW entered upon his military career at the age of 14 at the Junior Military Academy in Tokyo. He showed considerable ability and following his graduation from the Military Academy served as both student and instructor at various service schools. While on Saipan he heard that he had been promoted to Lieutenant Colonel but was captured before he received official notification of this.

PW's long experience with artillery, both as student and teacher, suggested a thorough interrogation on Japanese artillery doctrine. PW has revealed a keen intelligence which warrants the belief that his discussion of his specialty represents the theories and practice of the better Japanese artillery officers. Moreover, as far as can be checked, PW's statements appear reliable.

PW's character also confirms the impression of the reliability of what he has to say. He is sufficiently realistic to recognize that Japan has lost. The sensible thing, he feels, is therefore to end the war and to this end he is willing to assist American intelligence. He believes, further, that there will be an opportunity in post-war Japan for those who have the confidence of the Allies. Moreover, as much on account of their incompetence as anything else, he has no love for the military hierarchy.

PW entered the army not through inclination but because of parental insistence and accordingly never was at home in his military career. His primary interests lay in foreign affairs and western culture, to which he brings a fairly fluent knowledge of both English and French. These inclinations produced a rather liberal sophistication that did not fit in army circles.

2. ORGANIZATION

New Division Organization.

PW made the following comments upon the Japanese "streamlined" division.

The so-called "streamlined" division was organized only for the purposes of island defense. A compact, more heavily armed division was felt best suited to the requirements of war in the Pacific. This type of reorganization were placed in depot divisions.

The formation of regimental combat teams in which the artillery battalion comes under the exclusive control of the infantry regimental commander resulted from the feeling of the infantry commanders that they should be given full control of the tactical usage of artillery fire. (PW opposed this move, maintaining that artillery would lose much of its effectiveness if placed in the hands of infantry commanders.) Artillery regiments have not been broken up except in the formation of "streamlined" divisions. Divisions in Japan, the Asiatic theaters and the Philippines retain divisional artillery regiment.

Amphibious regiments, which often supplant one infantry regiment in a "streamlined" division, were created as forces to effect counterlandings. One amphibious regiment may be expected in each group of islands, the theory being that the regiment can relieve any one of the islands which may be attacked. Amphibious units of regimental size are also found as independent units under Army Headquarters in Java, Timor and the Philippines.

Infantry Battalion Organization.

A general re-organization of the infantry battalion has taken place with the exception of units in Japan and some units in Manchuria. All battalions in southeast Asia, the Philippines and about 80% of the battalions in China have been re-organized as follows, a re-organization which PW states follows the current Russian pattern:

Bn Hq
90 — 100

Rifle Co	Rifle Co		Rifle Co	MG Co
120-30	same		same	170-5

HQ

1st Plat

2nd Plat

3rd Plat

HQ

1st Plat
4 HMG

2nd Plat
4 HMG

3rd Plat
4 HMG

4th Plat
Ammo Sect.

Total Personnel 620 — 665

There is no infantry gun company or mortar platoon regularly attached to this type of battalion. Two gun companies and a mortar company are attached to the regiment. In some cases, such as in units engaged in punitive expeditions, a gun company may be temporarily attached to the battalion. This type of battalion organization is distinguished from that found in the "streamlined" division in the retention of the three-platoon rifle company instead of a four-platoon company and in that the fourth company of the battalion is an MG company rather than an infantry gun company.

3. TRAINING & OPERATIONS

ARTILLERY TACTICS

The following comments are based on many interviews and map problems conducted with PW. During most of these problems he acted as commander of an artillery battalion supporting an infantry regiment. It is believed PW is representative of a high caliber professional Japanese artillery officer and that he reflected in his actions during these map exercises, standard Japanese artillery doctrines. Through these map exercises, the interrogator's questions were so framed as to make the PW "carry the ball".

Selection of Position.

Given the mission (direct support of an infantry regiment in an attack) he invariably would bring his batteries into position "well-forward" frequently to within 2,000 yards of his infantry front. He preferred night displacements and would usually make a personal reconnaissance of the areas. He normally took his battery commanders with him on his reconnaissance and assigned the general position areas for each battery. The battery commander then selected the specific position for his guns, OP's and horses. The horses were given an area about 1,000 yards in rear of the battery position. Defiladed positions for the guns were selected whenever possible. Distance between flank batteries varied according to the terrain and the disposition of infantry forces. The artillery battalion was expected to cover a front of about 2,000 to 2500 yards. During retrograde movements of the artillery, the battery and battalion commanders always stayed with their units while the battalion executive and other battery officers took care of reconnoitering positions.

Communications.

When the battalion commander went forward on reconnaissance his communications officer was always a member of his "party". Wire between the batteries and the battalion OP was laid as soon as positions had been selected and alternate communications in form of heliographs or semaphore were always up. A pool of five 3-A "walkie talkie" type radios, normal battalion signal equipment, was kept for use as alternate means of communication, or for use of any liaison personnel or forward observers that might be required. The primary means of communication within the battalion was wire and not radio.

Survey.

The battalion observation officer (who is also survey officer) also was a member of the battalion commander's reconnaissance party. If the battalion headquarters had qualified enlisted personnel, survey, under the direction of the observation officer, was started immediately. This survey crew would normally try to survey in three battalion OP's, the battery positions, orienting lines and two or three battalion base points. The battalion base points selected were at least 100 mils apart.

PW pointed out several times that most of their surveys were simple and not as accurate as they could be due to lack of personnel. When field artillery units are located near coastal defense units (as on the islands), these coastal defense units sometimes do the survey work for the field artillery since they are often more liberally equipped with skilled instrument men.

Firing Charts.

Each battery as well as the battalion begins a firing chart as soon as survey data becomes available. Two examples of battery firing charts are illustrated.

The battalion firing chart is kept by the observation officer under close supervision of the battalion commander. PW was wholly ignorant of the idea of a fire direction center as we know it and had never heard of anything like a graphical firing table, HCO or VCO. When questioned as to how he would mass the fire of his batteries on a single target area, he stated that it would be done by informing his battery commanders of the coordinates of the area, give each battery a sector of the area and then have them fire. Most of the time, each battery would register on the new target area before going into fire for effect.

PW stated that a fire direction set-up such as ours would undoubtedly permit them to shift battalion fires more accurately and rapidly but that lack of capable enlisted personnel and junior officers made such a thing difficult to accomplish.

Observation.

Habitually three battalion OP's as well as alternate OP's are established - one axial and two flank positions. If the target area is visible from these OP's, forward observers are not sent out. The artillery battalion tables of organization do not call for officer forward observers. If elevated OP's are not available then the battalion observation officer or one of the spare junior officers might go forward as an observer using the "walkie talkie" for communications.

Infantry-Artillery Liaison.

During an operation the artillery battalion commander sends one of his spare junior officers to the regimental infantry CP to act as liaison officer. PW stated that because of the difference in rank between the artillery liaison officer and the infantry regimental commander, the artillery lieutenant usually had a very difficult time in keeping up with the infantry situation and that, as a result, liaison between artillery and infantry was not all that it should be. Also, many infantry commanders were reluctant to ask for artillery support feeling that the infantry could take care of things by itself.

The same was true in the relation between the artillery batteries and the infantry battalion they were supposed to support. The battery-infantry battalion liaison consisted of an NCO from the battery who located himself at the infantry battalion CP.

DEFENSE OF AN ISLAND

The plan for the role of artillery in the defense of Saipan had been predicated on the use of prepared gun positions for protection against bombardment and on mobility to enable artillery units to make rapid displacements to these prepared positions.

The disposition of artillery units just prior to our landings were so situated as to be able to cover the three possible landing areas – the east, south and west shores of the island. The initial position areas appear to have been excellent with the OP's providing a birds-eye view of the entire target area. Communications and liaison were initially based on the utilization of the commercial telephone lines of the South Seas Development Company, supplemented by their own tactical nets.

By way of firing preparation, all units had registered on the beach areas and on buoys located at the approaches to the beach.

Radio communications for battalions and smaller units were very limited if not entirely absent. These units apparently had the radio sets, but the crystals which were to be used in these sets had been lost at sea when the ship carrying them had been sunk by submarines.

This artillery plan broke down early in the operation.

In the first place an insufficient number of prepared positions had been made. PW bitterly criticised the navy for its failure to build such positions. He stated that by the time the army units took over, it was too late to do much along that line because of the sinking of ships carrying the necessary materials -- cement, steel and the like.

Due to the lack of time, wire lines had not been buried deep enough or sometimes not at all (as in use of the commercial lines). As a result of this, the naval and air bombardment almost completely destroyed communications; thus vanished the means of achieving cooperative effort by the units. Centralized control over firing disappeared as did means for liaison between infantry and artillery. In one case it took half an hour for the battery to receive orders for a firing mission given by the artillery commander.

The absence of prime movers for the guns resulted in the abandonment or capture of these weapons in their original positions. Trucks had been used to bring the guns forward to these positions but they did not belong to the artillery. They were used primarily for hauling supplies. No horses were brought to Saipan because it had been discovered, when using them in places like Formosa, that they were of little use in this climate and terrain. Also the lack of shipping space would have precluded their use.

PW stated that the following factors were responsible for the breakdown of their artillery plans:

1. Lack of a sufficient amount of artillery. PW said that prior to our landings, each battalion had been assigned a sector of about 4,000 yards to cover. This was entirely too much. He believes they should have had at least twice as much artillery as they did.

2. Destruction of communication by our bombardments.

3. Lack of sufficiently prepared, fortified artillery positions.

4. Lack of prime movers which destroyed the mobility of the artillery and made it impossible to displace it in support of troops in critical areas.

When asked if he would have changed the location of the artillery battalion had he been in a position to do so, PW stated that he would have moved the second and third battalions west because of the dead space created by the hill located northwest of the position. Also, he would have spread out the batteries much more as a protective measure against the bombardment. The first artillery battalion should have been spread out so as to cover better a larger area. When asked about the artillery pieces found on and near the beach, PW stated that they were the infantry cannon; he had not seen them in position but had been informed that four 75mm infantry guns were set up to cover the landings with direct flanking fire.

Concerning the liaison between the army and navy units on Saipan, PW stated that the relationship between these units was very poor. Admiral Noguma and General Saito did not see eye to eye on many things and this relationship carried on down to the lower units. As to cooperation between the coastal guns and the field artillery, PW stated that there was apparently no one in direct command of the coastal guns and that they were fired at will by the individual gun commanders.

When asked about Japanese counter-battery fire on Saipan, he stated that as far as he knew they used no counter-battery because the American artillery decimated Japanese batteries before they could fire back. When questioned as to how the Japanese do counter-battery at night, he stated that they do not use night counter-battery fire except against those targets on which they had fired during the daytime.

DEFECTS OF JAPANESE ARTILLERY

PW stated that the deficiencies in Japanese field artillery were due to the following factors:

1. A lack of artillery materiel due to the limitation of Japan's industries and the emphasis on production of more critically needed items - particularly aircraft.

2. The inadequate performance of the 75mm howitzer which is the numerically predominant light artillery weapon. The Japanese artillery men would like to see these replaced with their 10cm howitzer but thus far production difficulties as mentioned above preclude any such changeover in the near future.

3. The lack of adequate field training, especially combined infantry-artillery maneuvers, resulting in a failure of officers of both arms fully to appreciate their interdependence in actual operations. Together with the "branch consciousness" of Japanese officers, this factor has frequently resulted in unsound tactical employment of artillery. Too many officers have had little actual field experience with troops due to the fact that the emphasis in training artillery officers has been on regarding the artillery as a separate arm and disregarding, to a large extent, the infantry-artillery relationship. Only very recently has there been very much practical emphasis on such subjects as liaison, forward observers with the infantry and, generally, the development of a closer relationship between the combined arms.

4. The all-around retarded development of field artillery. For example, PW stated that the artillerymen had been begging for aerial observation to augment their ground observation methods and finally were given some observation balloons (in China). This was about two years ago.

More recently the Field Artillery School had been experimenting with the use of a light low-performance airplane to be used for artillery observation. As far as he knew, these planes had not yet been used in actual operations to any extent but artillery officers were being trained at the Field Artillery School in conducting artillery fire from airplanes. They were able to use observation balloons in operations against the Chinese because they had air superiority. The great predominance of horse-drawn artillery, he stated, was another factor which had retarded development of the artillery. About the only mechanized (truck-drawn) artillery they had was on the mainland of China and Manchuria, but even there, only a very few units were thus equipped. He did not know specifically which units they were.

TRAINING OF JAPANESE ARTILLERY OFFICERS

The following deals with the training of key artillery officers -- battery, battalion and regimental commanders - most of whom are regular army officers and, as such, have received considerably more training than the bulk of field artillery officers.

Middle School (High School) graduates are eligible to take entrance examinations for the officer candidate schools. The duration of these schools has varied from two years (before the war) to about six months at the present time. At the time of entrance, the student chooses the branch of service he prefers. About 20% choose either artillery or engineers; most of the others selecting either the air corps or the infantry.

The artillery course is divided into observation and survey, communications, gunnery and tactics. About half of the time is devoted to field work, including much service practice. In general, this course covers about the same ground that our own Field Artillery School does; except, of course, that the subjects concerned with the fire direction center are missing.

On graduation, the student is assigned to a field unit as a probationary officer. Here he serves as a platoon commander, communications officer or assistant observation officer; and after six months of such duty receives his commission.

At this point, the young officer can take the examinations for a regular army commission, depending on his commanding officer's recommendations and on his record at the officer candidate school. Only a very small percentage of officers are accepted and from this group come most of the future artillery unit commanders. After becoming a regular, the officer is sent to the Artillery-Engineer School for one year's intensive work in mathematics and the physical sciences. The instructors are civilians and no strictly military subjects are covered. After completing this school, the officer returned to his unit and is then eligible after six months of field duty for the Field Artillery School at Chiba City, for advanced work in Field Artillery. The officer selects one of the following courses offered:

1. Materiel.
2. Conduct of fire and survey.
3. Gunnery.
4. Transportation.

PW considers the conduct of fire and the gunnery courses the best and most popular. Conduct of fire includes small and large "T", ricochet and time fire. All types of ground and aerial observation methods are covered.

In all firing, much importance is attached to the problems incident to obtaining good observation. Instruction at the Field Artillery School is centered about French Artillery doctrines for which the Japanese have a very high regard. PW stated that it was his ambition and the ambition of many other artillery officers before the war to be sent to Saint Cyr for more artillery training.

PW stated that German artillery officers have never been used as instructors at the Japanese Field Artillery School.

The PW was very proud of being an artillery officer and stated that the artillery and engineer officers in the Japanese army had a very high standing. From the ranks' of Japanese artillery officers have come many high ranking military leaders including Field Marshall Hata, Shunroku, Lieutenant General Kimura, Hyotaro, Lieutenant Sato, Kenryo and Lieutenant General Shimomura.

PW stated that the Japanese army was short of artillery officers. He estimated that about 300 new artillery officers are turned out each year from all sources and stated that they had needed about a 1,000 new artillery officers yearly because of the expansion of the army in China. One reason for the shortage was that at present the air force has a priority on all men who are officer material and takes all prospective officer candidates into this branch of service if they are physically qualified.

ARTILLERY - MISCELLANEOUS

1. Japanese artillery units down to battalions and in some cases batteries are equipped with the necessary thermometers, barometric guages and anemometers for securing their own "mif-mif" data.

2. The Japanese do not have any tank destroyer units as such. PW stated that the 37's and 47's found in the infantry regimental cannon company together with the infantry cannon were used as antitank weapons. He had heard that a 57 AT gun had been put out, but had not seen one. The members of the infantry cannon companies are trained in antitank fire. The procedure, he stated, was to hold fire until the tanks had reached a spot which had been "targeted in" and then to fire as rapidly as possible. The maximum range at which these guns opened up was, he stated, 1,000 meters.

3. The Japanese army has three observation regiments. Two of these are located in Manchuria and one in Japan. The functions of these units are to make and disseminate meteorological observations and to do survey work for artillery units in nearby areas. Since there are so few observation regiments, they cannot furnish data to all artillery units that request it. To remedy this situation it had been planned to assign six or eight man crews with instruments from the observation regiments to the artillery regiments. PW doubts that this plan has been put into effect because of the great shortage of men qualified for that type of work.

The observation regiments are equipped with a photo section for making obliques. PW stated that instruction at the Field Artillery School covered the methods of making true scale charts from the oblique photos but that this was practically never done in the field.

4. Richochet and time fire although taught at the artillery school, are seldom used in the field because time fuzes are hard to get (PW stated that no artillery time fuzes had been made for more than a year) and richochet fire is too unpredictable and hard to control and adjust.

5. Battery Organization.

The three-gun battery has replaced the four-gun battery in all areas except Japan and Manchuria. About 20% of the artillery units in China still

retained the four-gun battery at the beginning of this year but it is probable
that these have now been reduced to three-gun batteries. This move was
carried out in order to equally distribute Japan's dwindling supply of guns
and also, POW thinks, to effect triangulation of all possible elements.

6. Artillery Mortars.

The artillery mortar (Kyuho) battalion generally consists of two
batteries of one 250mm mortars apiece. In some cases, the battalion may consist of three 150mm mortars. The artillery mortar battalion is attached to
a regiment differing in this respect from a mortar battalion (Hakugekoho
Daitai) which is usually attached to army headquarters.

EXPEDITIONARY UNITS (HAKENTAI)

Expeditionary units were formed to obtain trained troops for island
defense. These units superceded garrison forces (Shubitai); however, this
was practically a change in name only. Expeditionary units of somewhat less
than regiment size were formed by combining three battalions from each of
three divisions or by combining three independent infantry battalions. This
method was adopted in order to avoid substantially reducing the strength of
any one division. Unless the division concerned were in Manchuria or Japan
no attempt was made to replace the missing battalions. Consequently, some
divisions in China are now understrength with one or more regiments of only
two battalions. PW has heard of the formation of only nine expeditionary
units and believes that this form or organization has been abandoned.

INFANTRY GROUP HEADQUARTERS (HOHEIDAN)

PW states that infantry group headquarters are now present only
in some units in Japan. In some cases infantry group headquarters were
removed bodily from the divisions and incorporated in expeditionary units
as headquarters. Generally, they were simply disolved and their personnel
returned to their original units.

GENERAL STAFF COLLEGE (RIKUGUN DAIGAKU)

The course at the school covers strategy and tactics, a foreign
language and tactical map exercises. About 80 officers per year are graduated.
On graduation about 40% are assigned to combat units, 40% become instructors
and the remaining 20% are assigned to staff jobs at the War Department.

MORALE AND PROPAGANDA

PW stated that conditions in the homeland, from which he departed
in May 1944, were comparatively little changed from those which prevailed
at the beginning of the war. Everything was rationed by a ticket system but
the stores were completely unable to provide even the small amount which was
authorized. Lines in front of the various stores formed early in the
morning and continued through the day. After waiting half a day or more in
line, the housewife could only obtain a very small amount of whatever was
being sold and usually this amount being insufficient to keep the family
for even one day. It was necessary to go to two or more shops. Those who
could afford maids were able to carry on, but in a household without a

maid the housewife spent her entire time standing in one line or another and as a result was unable to attend to her other household duties.

Soldiers' families did not receive special ration tickets or special privileges but the soldier could purchase certain items such as tobacco, beer and other similar items from his own canteen and take them home for the family. Officers who ate at home and hence bought their own food were the same as everyone else and no special privilege was given because of their officer status.

Intensive preparations were made for air raids and firebreaks were cut in many parts of Tokyo. Air raid drills were held constantly and preparations were considered adequate. However, in fact, the preparations were very superficial and not satisfactory for any large-scale attack. Practically every family has constructed its own air raid shelter but for the most part these shelters consist of merely a shallow hole in the ground with little or no covering overhead. Normally, in most parts of Tokyo deep shelters could not be dug because of the fact that water was fairly close to the surface. This applies particularly to the reclaimed ground on which portions of the city are built. The War and Navy Departments built large underground concrete dugouts and air raid shelters near their buildings in the capital. Construction was started just prior to the beginning of the war and completed shortly afterward. A small part of the population of Tokyo have been removed to the country and all who were not considered essential were advised to go to the country and live with relatives. This advice did not produce much response on the part of the people and the population is little changed.

The relationship between the services is not at all good. There is a great deal of friction between the army and navy and each attempts to blame its failures on some shortcoming of the other. The navy lives in grand style and has all kinds of supplies and equipment while the army has practically nothing. This gives rise to much bitter criticism of the navy by army personnel. The navy practically runs the entire show in the Pacific area and army troops operating under them are not given the same priviliges, supplies and facilities that navy troops have, which is a source of dissatification and grumbling.

On Saipan, commodities were not rationed. However, due to the fact that it served as a supply base for practically the whole of the southern areas, supplies for the local inhabitants were inadequate, the greater part being shipped on to other places. Relations between the services and the local people were normally good.

PW states that Bushido is essentially the same as western chivalry; however, the military clique in Japan has distorted it to their own purposes and ruined its real significance. In the event of defeat or American landings on Japan proper, PW does not believe that the Japanese civilians will commit suicide in large numbers. Undoubtedly there will be some suicides but the number will be comparatively small and the Japanese civilian can be very simple handled by those who know modern Japan.

The Japanese policy of resistance unto death is something that is taught from childhood according to the principles of Buddhism. Buddhism teaches that, even though a person dies in unsuccessful battle, he will go to heaven and there will be able to win this battle. In other words, his failure in this life will be turned into sure success in the next one. This teaching is one of the motivating factors of the Banzai charges and suicides which occur from time to time and it is quite difficult to rationalize against this lifetime of training, as such beliefs are so thoroughly imbued in the average Japanese that they cannot be questioned.

PW drew the following example of Japan's attitude toward the war: He says that it is the same as a starving man who has ten dollars with which to purchase food. He is very hungry and his stomach is crying to be filled. As a result, he buys the entire ten dollars worth of food and stuffs it down at one time, thereby satisfying his immediate need with no thought of the future in spite of the fact that he does not know where his next meal is coming from.

PW believes that it is a fallacy to say that PWs cannot return to Japan after the war. Such a belief is, of course, derived from the fact that much disgrace is heaped upon those who surrender and returned prisoners are subject to court martial. However, if Japan is decisively defeated, as PW thinks she will be, all of the people will be in the same class and no special stigma can be placed on any particular PW.

PW is an interested follower of the progress of the war and devotes his spare time to the study of English. He has aspiration of being given a good position in Japan in conjunction with the American military government which he contemplates will be set up. He thinks that he will have ample opportunity to be of service to the occupation authorities as well as his country. He desires to devote himself to the service of mankind and explains this feeling by saying that his patriotism has become "scientific". PW believes that there is a slight possibility that the military clique will flee to Manchuria and endeavor to carry on resistance from there, but if this should take place it will be without the support of the common people and will be doomed to failure, as PW feels that Manchuria cannot produce enough armament and supplies to keep an army supplied.

Propaganda for the homeland should be divided into three classes:

1. The "little people" such as farmers, workers, fisherman, etc.
2. Students.
3. The higher and official class.

The standard of education of the "little people" is very low and in addressing propaganda to them, very simple Japanese should be used. There is, of course, a happy medium which can be reached. It must be simple without appearing to be childish or ridiculous. In general, actual photographs of large groups of prisoners with their faces indistinguishable and photographs of falling planes and sinking ships are thought to be the most effective.

PW believes that propaganda will be effective if continued for a long period of time and the proper build-up given to outright surrender appeals. He does not believe that any propaganda is effective until circumstances become very unfavorable for the troops. However, if propaganda is not used until this time, it will not be effective except in rare cases because of the inability to absorb new ideas under the stress of battle conditions. In other words, propaganda attempts should be made at the earliest possible date to expose the troops to these new ideas and allow them time to absorb and assimilate them thoroughly before the battle starts. The leaflets will be read and remembered and when conditions become difficult, the follow-up of new and additional surrender propaganda will then be received with more favor.

News sheets of all kinds are thought to be very effective in that the soldier in the field normally has little, if any, access to news of any kind. A steady supply of news sheets dropped periodically on the troops would do much to pave the way for the further reception of other propaganda.

WASTAGE AND CASUALTIES

Disposition of Troops Surviving Sinkings en route to Saipan.

The large number of troops who arrived at Saipan as surviviors of ship sinkings presented an apparently insoluble problem to army headquarters. There was an attempt at a makeshift reorganization following their original T/O's but this plan had not progressed to any extent at the time of our landing. Spare rifles and other equipment were gathered and stored on the grounds of the South Seas Development Company preparatory to issuing them to these troops but, again, this plan was forestalled by our landings. Consequently, these troops were left to their own devices, some obtaining rifles from the dump and joining organized units, while other unarmed, did little but get in the way.

SPECIAL INTELLIGENCE

Army - Navy Liaison.

There was, for all practical purposes, no cooperation between army and navy units on Saipan. Inter-service jealousy and the feeling among army officers that naval troops were not qualified for land warfare seems to have been responsible for this situation. After army headquarters orders had been disregarded by the naval land troops there was no further attempt at any sort of liaison.

REPORT ON CAVALRY RECONNAISSANCE SQUADRON
MECHANIZED

Mounted and Dismounted Employment.

The tactical employment of this unit has been approximately half dismounted action.

The reconnaissance squadron must be rapidly and easily converted, to any degree of combination from mounted to dismounted action. Occasions of particularly rapid developments have required that complete conversion be made within a space of a very few hours. The ease with which this conversion can be accomplished depends entirely upon the precombat training and the combat employment of the squadron in that combination role in the attack and the defense.

A greater percentage of the precombat training of this unit was in the mounted work. Consequently, when first actually in combat there was a reluctance among the troops to dismount and continue forward dismounted. Constant necessity and practice in combat has proven the worth and any reluctance has been removed allowing the unit to be more fluid than any other unit of equal size.

Lessons Learned and Trends.

Strictest of discipline in soldiering, maintenance, supply, training and teamwork are essential. Any degree short of near perfection is a waste of manpower and material.

"Sneak and peak" reconnaissance is very good if it is possible. It is seldom possible. Experience has shown that boldness, tempered with caution and common sense used to fight for information gets results. Temerity or hesitancy in the face of ordinary delaying action will result in no information and no advance.

A thorough knowledge and study of maps and aerial photographs are essential for accurate reconnaissance. The responsibility for an error in location affects not only the platoon or troop involved, but the corps plans because corps depends on the reconnaissance squadron for absolutely accurate information.

Changes in Doctrine.

The former tendency for a reconnaissance squadron to depend mostly on mounted reconnaissance has been found to be incorrect in this theater. Good reconnaissance will be accomplished when a coordinated mounted, dismounted, and air team is designed and trained as a unit. It should be created, used and trained as a team because such a trained team only is capable of over-coming the confusion caused by the strain of fierce combat.

The assault guns are used either in battery or attached, by platoon to the reconnaissance troops. Usually, where the situation is mobile and the reconnaissance troops are widely separated, the assault guns are attached for support and are fired by forward reconnaissance platoons on targets of opportunity using radio for communications and reconnaissance platoon leaders to sense the fire. Whenever the squadron is employed in a defensive section, the assault guns are set up in battery, wired for telephone fired in on defensive concentrations and are fired by the assault gun platoon leaders from OP's through the troop "fire direction center".

The prompt recording, action and file of every telephone and written message received day or night within this squadron has been found to pay valuable dividends. In this way messages are properly coordinated with the bulk of information received and therefore can be properly evaluated.

BATTLE
PATROL

Note: The "battle patrol" described herein is fairly typical of those organized by a number of infantry regiments. Practically all units using such groups employ special measures to build up the morale of the group and enhance the desirability of being a member.
Comments of an infantry regimental S-2:

1. Composition and privileges: "We have organized a "battle patrol" unit which performs patrol and special combat missions and supplements the work of the intelligence and reconnaissance platoons. All men are volunteers generally between the ages of 18 and 24. They work, play and sleep together. They do no guard or kitchen police and have no other duties when not on patrol. They receive three hot meals a day when not in action and hot baths frequently. We are also procuring special insignia for them.

2. Organization and equipment: "The patrol is organized into seven squads of five men each. The headquarters consists of one officer, a platoon sergeant, a supply sergeant and two operations clerks. Each man has his normal weapon and, in addition, we have made available to the patrol, four bazookas, 10 automatic rifles, 12 M-3 submachine guns and a light machine gun. Arms carried on a particular raid or patrol depend upon the mission. Fifteen clips are carried for each browning automatic rifle.

3. Training: "We gave the patrol several weeks special training before its first action. Its good results are due mainly to good teamwork, good morale and a very careful prior study and planning of each action.

4. Operations: "Prior to an action the patrol is carefully briefed and then taken to an observation post to study the terrain for about four hours. They are then brought back, fed a hot meal, briefed again and any troubles or uncertainties cleared up. When we send out a number of 'teams' from a patrol, we generally have one follow another so as to assist in case of trouble. We also use phase lines to control progress. When a single patrol is used one man stays at the observation post and four go forward. The "battle patrol" is available to any battalion which has a suitable mission for it.

5. Results:

a. "On one occasion patrols crossed the Saar River and remained behind the German line for 36 hours making reports by SCR-300. They paid particular attention to what they could see of our lines from their concealed position and among other things reported the flow of our traffic over an important Bailey bridge. Their reports caused us to delay the movement of some artillery because the bridge was under such good enemy observation,

b. "The patrol is sometimes given a mission to secure a particular objective and, in one case, successfully attacked a village held by a superior enemy force.

c. "Not many men of the patrol speak German but they are picking it up fast. One man, while a member of one of these patrols, captured six prisoners and managed to bring them back, in addition to some of our own wounded, directly through three German strong points. His success was due to his knowledge of German and his quick wit - he even prevailed upon a German sergeant to guide him through a mine field'."

COMMENTS OF AN ENGINEER COMBAT BATTALION ON THE ELIMINATION OF NOISE IN PATROL RIVER CROSSINGS

"Here's how we help infantry raiding parties across a river without the noise of paddling. Send a party across by swimming, carrying one end of a half-inch rope. The far shore party then can pull across the boats carrying the infantry. This eliminates the noise of a motor or of rowing. For more than one trip, attach ropes at each end of the boat and let the far and near shore parties pull it across in turn. Don't forget an infantry security detail for the far shore party."

REPORT ON PRISONER OF WAR RAID

"Thorough planning, coordinated supporting fires and rapid execution contributed to the success of a prisoner of war raid by a reconnaissance troop platoon. The objective, an enemy outpost across a river, was observed to be occupied each night. The plan for the raid was simple and the action was rehearsed. Before H-hour six men took positions on the near bank to cover the crossing. H-3, a light artillery battalion fired on the outpost and a medium battalion, together with 81mm and 60mm mortars boxed in the objective. At H-hour the light battalion fire lifted 200 yards to the rear of the objective, the boxing fire continued and two groups of six men each crossed the river at points 40 yards apart. On the far bank they formed quickly into a 50 yard skirmish line and moved to the objective. Three Germans were captured easily. A fourth, who reached for a machine gun, was killed. The raiders withdrew with the prisoners before enemy mortar and artillery fire came down on the area."

MOPPING UP OPERATION - ADMIRALTY ISLANDS

The Admiralty Islands campaign as conducted by the 1st Cavalry Division, closed on 18 May. At that time there was an estimated 1400 of the enemy still surviving. For the most part they were hiding in native gardens on the slopes of Mt. Dremsel, the dominating land mass of Manus, rising well over 2000 feet above the sea. Very little information was available on this section because of the forbidding nature of the terrain and because the inland natives had, with few exceptions, come down to the coast. The enemy at this time did not constitute a threat to the security of the Admiralty Islands but because of their harassing action against the natives; and to obviate any possible reaction to the extensive naval developments, it was deemed advisable that they be eliminated. This was also in accordance with the proposed training program, both for the experienced soldiers who had participated in the campaign and for the expected replacements.

Captured enemy documents indicated that the Jap survivors had been ordered to proceed to Kali Bay on the western coast of Manus Island. This was logical as there were ample native food supplies on Kali Island and evacuation from that point by submarine was remotely possible. Therefore Manus Island was divided into zones of action which were in turn subdivided by the units to which the zones were assigned. This zoning first provided that the enemy escape routes be blocked and secondly that the remaining portions of the island be given thorough coverage.

The start of the mopping up operations coincided with the arrival of the first replacements, who came to the 1st Cavalry Division directly from the United States. These replacements were immediately incorporated in the program within their assigned units.

Approximately one week was allotted for the orientation and re-equipment of the replacements. The orientation week included brief lectures by the most experienced patrol leaders in the unit. These lectures served the double purpose of inspiring confidence in the leaders and of providing each man with a complete understanding of the situation. Immediately following the week of orientation the replacements were sent to Manus for an extended period varying from three weeks to a month.

The organization, strength and composition of the patrols were in accordance with the three basic conceptions of patrols as included in the pre-figuration.

Long range patrolling over primary trails to cover an average of 20 miles in 4 days, and to include side trails and all known hideouts customarily used by the enemy. These were ordinarily 10-man patrols, habitually inclusive of 7 trainees and 3 experienced men. Duration of patrol; 6 days.

Close in patrols over secondary trails to cover completely the inexhaustible number of native trails in a relatively small given area. This type patrol naturally stressed a painstaking search for any evidence of previous Jap occupation and also sought out any prospective hideouts and suitable locations for ambush. Twelve men operated together in these patrols with an average proportion of two replacements for each experienced man.

Ambush: Based on native reports and previous patrol results, ambushes were established on primary trail junctions and at principal food sources. These patrols, which did not exceed a strength of five men, concentrated on extreme patience, total immobility, the elimination of all evidence of their presence and complete familiarization with the immediate area to insure coverage of all possible approach and escape routes.

Roving patrols were subdivided to provide a three man point and a two man rearguard.

The BAR, which was so popular in combat, was abandoned on patrols as its weight was prohibitive and its firepower was not required. A few Thompson Sub-Machine Guns were carried but the carbine and M1 were the principal weapons. Each man carried two hand grenades. The important thing was to allow the individual to carry the weapon of his choosing consistent with the assigned mission.

Iron rations were used exclusively throughout the training period. Rations were broken down according to item prior to the start of the patrols. Cognizant of the length and type of the proposed patrol, each man carried what he personally desired. The types available, even though carried individually in packs for as much as seven days, proved satisfactory and adequate. Preference in rations was based on the fact that the patrols were allowed a hot noon meal involving the use of a fire. No fires were allowed either in the morning or evening.

The patrols operated from a base camp which was merely a resupply point and not a bivouac. An SCR 193 was used at this point for the transmittal of patrol reports to higher headquarters.

All patrol activities stressed paitence, stealth and thorough observation rather than the coverage of extensive areas. In this connection, great care was exercised in the approach to any suspected or known place of enemy concealment. The employment of three or four hours to cover the last one hundred yards was customary procedure. Certain Allied guides favored an immediate burst of fire as soon as the target was perceived by the leading elements, but as the percentage of escapees was too large following the employment of this method, it was immediately discarded as our patrols gained experience.

A complete reconnaissance was made not only of the target area but of all possible escape routes and nearby places of concealment. Two men customarily took up a position about one hundred yards from the target and so situated as to cover the trail most likely to be utilized for an attempted escape. The patrols were often forced to exercise great patience, in one case waiting over three hours for a dispersed group of the enemy to gather for their noon meal. In another instance, a three-man patrol, operating on a secondary mission for a larger patrol, employed two men to take a position of observation within twenty yards of the enemy, while the third man contacted and brought up the remainder of the patrol. These men remained in observation at this close range for an entire night and part of the next morning and upon arrival of the patrol leader, were able to furnish a minute description of the objective including the immediate composition and disposition of the individual enemy weapons.

Through the occasional employment of native guides, valuable knowledge in tracking the enemy was acquired. It was soon possible to determine by careful observation the strength of the enemy, the speed of his movement and by consideration of the distances between halts, his physical condition. The patrols also learned to examine the ground carefully for five or ten yards on either side of the trail intersections for on approaching a primary trail, the Jap's usual procedure was to cut across and come out above or below the intersection. This was also true of stream crossings.

- Another notable characteristic of the lone Japs who escaped from a fire fight was their tendency to take cover in the immediate vicinity of the action. In one case the lone survivor of a party of three Japs was found in hiding less than fifty yards from the scene of the action, although the patrol had delayed pursuit for fifteen minutes. This ruse nearly succeeded as the point of the patrol did not expect to find any Japs immediately after the action and were not proceeding with their usual thoroughness. Men to the rear of the column found the Jap less than three feet off the trail.

Toward the completion of the mopping up operations, the surviving enemy were faced with starvation. Taking advantage of this, food was left in strategic places while ambushes were set upon the approaches. One bag of rice placed on the stump of a tree at a trail intersection accounted for four Japs within two hours for the hungry enemy abandoned caution when the food was discovered.

The individual observation of the patrol members was emphasized. Upon the completion of each patrol, the patrol members were questioned separately. Care was taken to draw out the individual's interpretation of his observations. As a basic example, the discovery of an abandoned Jap rifle led to an interrogation as to the number of enemy in the group, whether or not they were taking care of their equipment and the proximity and direction of their last bivouac.

The concrete proof of the success of these tactics is evident in final casualty figures. 1383 of the enemy were killed and captured as compared to our losses of 2 KIA and 11 WIA over the total period of operations. The enormous value of this practical training of replacements was proven again and again in the operations of the 1st Cavalry Division in Leyte, Samar and Luzon.

SMALL-UNIT TACTICS USED BY JAPANESE AT NIGHT

1. Introduction:

Tactics used by Japanese companies and smaller units in night attacks are described below. This information, based on enemy sources, appears to be a fairly complete summary.

In the paraphrased Japanese manual which follows, particular attention should be paid to the enemy's reconnaissance methods, his massing of forces (the main body) in the approach march and during the early stages of the assault and his reliance upon the bayonet in rushing hostile position.

2. The Manual:

a. Preparations:

Upon receiving orders for a night attack, company commanders acquaint their platoon leaders with the major points of the plan. Preparations are begun, with special emphasis placed on gaining a thorough knowledge of the terrain and on the disposition of hostile forces.

The thoroughness of preparations will depend upon the situation. If there is an interval of several days between the formation of plans and the actual attack, successive patrols will be sent out - at least one of them during darkness.

b. Reconnaissance:

Knowledge of the terrain and of hostile dispositions is normally gained by reconnaissance patrols, each of which consist of five or six men (never more than ten). A reconnaissance by a small patrol led by an officer is considered highly desirable before a night attack.

Forward lookout posts are then established for the purpose of observing new developments. If necessary, these are investigated, in turn, by additional officer-led patrols. The company commander also makes forward observations and his headquarters personnel maintains a continuous lookout.

In reconnoitering, our patrols get as close as possible to the hostile positions and try to induce the opposing forces to fire or to attack so that they will reveal their strength and their positions. If possible, our patrols fix the exact location of these positions by measuring their distance and direction from some easily recognized terrain feature.

The reconnaissance also determines the type, strength and location of obstacles to be met in the night attack. Outguards, flanking machine-gun positions and illumination methods are noted. Nearby terrain is inspected. Subordinate leaders familiarize themselves, under night conditions, with the hostile positions and the terrain involved. If possible the entire unit which is to take part in the attack is given the opportunity to view, from a vantage point, the terrain over which the attack will move.

Normally, soon after dusk on the night of the attack, a patrol goes out to lay out the approach route, which, to the greatest possible extent, follows continuous terrain features in the desired direction. Roads, railroads, telegraph lines and ridge lines or other topographical features are thus used to maintain direction at night. The approach route is usually marked with pieces of white paper or cloth or personnel may be stationed as markers. Ropes may be stretched along the route and distances paced off.

c. The Approach:

In the approach march, the company advances in a line of columns but other formations are used freely to cope with special situations. Within the company, the squads move in a very close formation, with the minimum distance between men. The men may advance with a hand on the shoulder of the soldier in front. Also they may advance at a crouching walk.

When the company is attacking independently, patrols provide all-around protection. They usually are 30 to 50 yards from the main force, depending on visibility and on the nature of the terrain. If the company is advancing as part of a battalion, patrols are sent out to assigned sectors to the front. They are instructed to rush small groups of hostile forces, such as sentires and outpost personnel. Groups which the patrols cannot handle are dealt with by a small advance force, previously designated for such emergencies. Meanwhile the main body of the company continues its advance and takes no part in these preliminary actions.

The company maintains liaison with battalion headquarters by means of runners but it also takes individual responsibility for maintaining the direction of advance necessary to reach its objective even if contact with the battalion is lost. To maintain proper contact and direction, the company uses connecting files between the advance guard and the main body.

In addition to the various methods of maintaining direction which are outlined before the attack, compasses and stars are used for orientation. Flares of different colors may be fired at times and places designated in advance. Pairs of lights may be set out to the rear; when these lights are lined up they indicate the correct direction. As a rule, some of the personnel of the patrols used in earlier reconnaissance serve as guides (the others accompany the main force) and show the way by flashing signals to the rear with a shaded flashlight.

The company commander moves at the head of his force, giving orders by signal (flags or white cloths). Heavy weapons advance behind the company since they are rarely used for the attack but are needed in defending captured positions. Sometimes these weapons are used to fire on hostile illuminating equipment. Light machine guns are kept well to the rear of each squad. Automatic guns (antitank rifles) are usually left in the rear since tanks are not likely to be encountered at night. Pack horses for the automatic guns and for the heavy weapons usually remain with the ammunition platoon.

The company reserve, usually a platoon, is kept in readiness to counter any enemy (United Nations) attempt to surround our attacking forces or else the reserve may execute a flank attack on the objective if the frontal assault by the main force bogs down.

The approach march ends at a previously selected point and the company pauses briefly to complete preparations for the final assault. This point is as close as possible to the hostile forces - usually about 300 yards on ordinary terrain. Here, final contact with forward patrols is made, final details regarding demolitions are decided upon and final dispositions for the assault are carried out.

Absolute secrecy and quiet are enforced prior to an attack. Commands are given by signal only. Lights are concealed and are used only for signaling purposes. Camouflage is used even after dark and precautions against hostile patrols or spies are redoubled. Personnel usually wear white cloths for identification and the countersigns are drilled into every man.

d. Demolitions:

Detailed plans for demolishing obstacles are worked out on the basis of information obtained by reconnaissance and observation.

For ordinary demolitions such as the task of cutting a gap in barbed wire, a few men from each platoon are designated. If sturdy obstructions, such as pillboxes, must be overcome, a detachment of engineers (about 15 men) will be assigned to perform the task under the direction of the company commander. These engineers are demolition experts equipped with Bangalore torpedoes and mines.

Points where gaps in wire entanglements are to be cut usually are in areas easy to approach or in areas difficult for the opposition to cover with fire. In any case, the selection of these points is dictated chiefly by the plans for the attack. Gaps for night attacks are normally at closer intervals than those for day attacks.

Demolitions are completed just before the assault. Premature demolitions which might reveal the attack plans and allow time for repairs are avoided; however, allowance is made in time schedules for possible hostile interference.

Demolitions are executed as secretly as possible. Force is employed only when time is too short or hostile interference too great. If necessary, patrols are dispatched to protect demolition teams or to capture the point selected for demolition.

The time element involved in executing demolitions should be noted. Making a gap in barbed-wire entanglements 6 yards deep requires from 2 to 3 hours when the work is done by one man and from $1\frac{1}{2}$ to $2\frac{1}{2}$ hours when it is done by two men.

e. Assault:

From the position where the approach march has ended, the company moves out in a body as secretly as possible to within rushing distance of the opposing forces - crawling, if necessary. The company commander usually moves at the head of his unit, directing its full force and controlling his subordinates with positiveness. The rush is made with great energy, silently and without fire. The objective is taken by use of the bayonet.

If hostile forces are encountered before the main objective is reached they are dealt with by a detachment from the main body. A detachment may also be used to neutralize important pillboxes or other points of resistance to the attack.

Although effective hostile fire may stop our advance momentarily our forces determinedly try to continue - creeping or crawling and utilizing shadows. If our forces are near, they may close with the bayonet immediately after receiving fire. If they are too far away, they keep moving forward independently until close enough for the final rush.

(Observer's comment: The Japanese are especially afraid of being caught by fire while passing through the breeches in the wire. They probably are prepared either to cover this phase with smoke or to send patrols ahead to cover the main body while traversing the wire. If it appears necessary to reduce troublesome pillboxes or to repel small counterattacks during the final assault units are designated to take care of these tasks.

In dealing with pillboxes, the Japs stress surprise and deception and employ varied and original ideas for the latter. Smoke, dummy soldiers, gun flashes or small forces operating in the opposite direction from the attack are standard stratagems. To overcome the defenders, assault from the rear is preferred.

Under some circumstances, the Japanese may be expected to use only a part of the company to seize the objective, afterwards holding it with the whole force. When opposition at the objective is small and when there is likelihood of hostile fire from outside the defended position, it is not considered advantageous to expose the entire company unnecessarily. And where some terrain feature makes possible a surprise attack and breakthrough by a smaller group it is thought better to hold back the main force whose movements might be hampered by this same terrain. In every case the company commander leads the attacking force in person.)

f. Reorganization:

Once the objective has been gained the company halts and reorganizes. Patrols are dispatched immediately to pursue the hostile forces and reconnoiter their rear positions and the terrain to the rear. Dispositions are made to repel counterattacks and fire power is sited for close-range use. However, hand-to-hand fighting is preferred wherever possible and weapons are not loaded without orders from the company commander. Platoons automatically send out all-around security patrols. If the ground is to be held permanently they may change positions before daybreak to limit damage from hostile air and artillery attack.

Any hostile forces remaining in the vicinity are mopped up. If necessary, the whole company is used for this task. Dispositions for defense and security measures are supervised by the company commander himself.

SOUVENIR HUNTING IS STILL A PROBLEM

Souvenir hunting in combat zones continues to be a matter requiring caution. It is perhaps hard for some men to realize that a scrap of paper or a small metal plate with a few words in a foreign language on it can be of great ultimate significance in analyzing the military and economic resources of the enemy.

Because of the activities of souvenir hunters during operations on more than one Pacific island, much material of known and probable value was carried away and almost all enemy documents, personal papers, weapons and equipment were so rummaged through and scattered about that their eventual salvage was either unnecessarily delayed or rendered impossible. Souvenir hunting was not confined to any one unit or group but was undertaken by construction battalions, defense forces and ships' crews-personnel who came ashore after the assault phase had been completed. Not that there had been any lag between the assault and the beginning of the souvenir hunting. Even by mid-afternoon of the first day, considerable damage had been done, for houses, stores and barracks had been stripped almost as fast as they had been taken.

As experienced observers have pointed out, every effort must be made through training, indoctrination and briefing immediately before an operation, to minimize indiscriminate souvenir hunting and to insure the utmost cooperation between troops and construction units on one hand and intelligence personnel on the other

At present there is a vital need for every available name plate from enemy materiel of every description. It is essential that, whenever possible the name plate be left on the captured equipment to which it pertains. In recent weeks an increasing number of loose name plates have been confiscated from the mails by censors. Although it is a War Department policy that military personnel be treated as generously as possible when they request permission to retain souvenirs, it is obvious that items of intelligence value must be held for examination by the proper authorities. Experience has shown again and again that the most trivial-looking items can reveal desperately needed information concerning the enemy.

Sometimes it has proved advisable to post guards over captured command posts, radio stations, supply dumps and so on, so that documents and materiel can be examined thoroughly without having been subjected to previous handling and the resulting damage and loss.

The responsibility for turning in for examination any random documents or pieces of equipment found by military personnel of course rests directly with the officers in charge of the various units involved in an operation.

The brighter side of the picture — and there very definitely is a brighter side — is illustrated by the following statement by a high-ranking U.S. officer who fought the Japanese on Rendova:

"If handled properly, souvenir collecting pays dividends; if not, it hurts morale and ruins an excellent source of information. Our rule was that a soldier could keep a souvenir if he were given clearance by his company commander, the intelligence officer and the ordnance officer. The men cooperated wonderfully and it was through 'souvenirs' brought in by collectors that we knew, two hours after we reached Rendova, the enemy's strength and disposition of troops over the previous two months' period."

OPERATION OF A DIVISION CIC DETACHMENT IN THE PHILIPPINES

1. Mission:

The counter intelligence corps detachment of a division operating under the direction of the assistant chief of staff G-2 of the division has a primary and a secondary mission.

    a. Primary Mission:

        (1) To detect and investigate all matters pertaining to espionage, sabotage, dissension and subversive activities occurring within the military organization.

        (2) To apprehend enemy agents or otherwise nullify their activities.

        (3) To inform proper authorities regarding the deficiencies in the security of vital civil and military installations.

        (4) To assist in the security instruction of military personnel in the field and during stabilized operations.

        (5) To assist in the combat area, to insure the security of captured enemy installations, documents and material.

b. Secondary Mission:

    (1) To collaborate with the civil affairs section in preparing security regulations and proclamations for the maintenance of order; control of civilian movement; assembly and publications; and curfew and blackout, where considered a military necessity.

    (2) To cooperate with the provost marshal in the operation of reception and interrogation points for non-Japanese personnel to determine nationality, citizenship and knowledge of matters significant to the prosecution of the war.

    (3) To search enemy headquarters, billets and any other installations likely to contain records and papers of intelligence value; supervising the collection and safeguarding of same.

    (4) To cooperate with the provost marshal in assuring the security of governmental offices.

    (5) To supervise civilian communications in captured territories, i.e., mail, telephone and telegraph until relieved by appropriate authority.

    (6) To aid in enforcing prescribed security regulations.

    (7) To arrest and interrogate known enemy agents and collaborators, arranging for their detention by the provost marshal.

    (8) To investigate and report enemy atrocities.

    (9) To establish informer networks among civilians and guerrillas, for counterintelligence and intelligence information.

    (10) To cooperate in the establishment of necessary identification and pass systems for civilian population.

    (11) To establish port security where necessary.

2. Organization:

a. General:

To discharge the mission outlined above the detachment was divided into the following sections:

    (1) Security Squad - Duty to search, seize and secure enemy dumps and installations, to secure enemy documents, maps, material, etc.

    (2) Investigation Squad - Duty to detain, secure evidence, interrogate and investigate alleged collaborators and spies.

    (3) Special Squad - To act as police squad to arrest and seize suspects.

    (4) Informers Net - Duty to secure and organize confidential informants.

    (5) Administrative Section - To perform the administrative duties of the detachment, clerical work, typing, maintenance of records, etc.

b. Personnel:

For this operation the detachment comprised the following personnel:

(1) 3 - officers.
(2) 17 - enlisted men. Included five (5) Filipinos and one (1) guerrilla agent.
(3) The detachment was supplemented by:

    (a) Civilian censorship unit - One (1) officer and one (1) enlisted man.
    (b) Military censorship unit - One (1) officer and one (1) enlisted man.

Rigid allocation of personnel to the sections of the detachment was not enforced. The personnel was applied according the urgency of the situation.

    c. Equipment:

Counter intelligence corps detachment - Three (3) ¾ ton 4x4, one (1) weapons carrier.
Civilian censorship unit - one (1) ¾ ton 4x4.
Military censorship unit - one (1) ¾ ton 4x4.
Necessary office equipment, files, records, etc.

    3. Operation:

    a. Personnel of the security section landed on the beach immediately after the assault elements and at once began a search for enemy dumps, materiel, documents, etc.

    b. Personnel of the detachment entered a large city along with the infantry on D/1. From data compiled prior to embarkation, five buildings were to be located and secured. These buildings were located, placed as "off limits" and guards posted for the night. The remainder of the detachment arrived in the city the morning of D/2, established counterintelligence corps headquarters and the organization prepared to function.

    c. Liaison established with assistant chief of staff G-2 at the division command post.

    d. Coordination procedures established with the provost marshal, military police, PCAU and civil affairs unit.

    e. Site of local compound selected.

    f. Local security established.

    g. Contact established with the organized guerrillas.

    4. Accomplishments:

    a. For several months prior to embarkation the operation of the counter intelligence corps detachment had been planned and a considerable amount of information had been secured from various sources as to possible enemy headquarters locations, dumps and the names of collaborators, puppet officials, Kempei agents, etc., totaling approximately three hundred (300) names in all.

b. In the opinion of the observer the following are accomplishments worthy of mention which were achieved by D/4:

    (1) Nineteen (19) enemy food dumps, located and turned over to PCAU.

    (2) Over eight hundred (800) individuals interrogated, cleared and turned over to PCAU.

    (3) One hundred and fifty-eight (158) of the individuals included on the original "black list" were picked up.

    (4) The names of forty-eight (48) additional suspects were added to the "black list" from information secured during interrogation of other prisoners.

    (5) Countless number of Japanese maps and documents secured from former Jap army and navy headquarters and the office and house of the Jap liaison officer to the area.

    (6) Eight (8) sworn affidavits as to enemy atrocities.

5. Comments:

a. The activities of the counter intelligence corps detachment in this operation was most interesting due primarily to the situation of the area itself, which included:

    (1) Unusual terrain features, rugged Jap defenses including their usual holes and caves.

    (2) Excellent harbor.

    (3) Number of adjacent islands, reports on which indicated the existence of Jap nationals or collaborators.

    (4) An established puppet government operating in conjunction with the Japanese.

    (5) An organized Filipino constabulary controlled by the Japs.

    (6) An organized Kempei unit.

    (7) A very well organized guerilla unit commanded by an American officer.

    (8) The existence of an unusual number of notable characters.

b. This detachment was commended on the manner in which prior planning was handled and also upon the efficient manner in which these plans were executed with a minimum of confusion and uncertainty.

RECONNAISSANCE TROOP IN THE LIBERATION OF GUAM

The employment of cavalry units in the jungle-clad islands and atolls of the Pacific have digressed many tactical furlongs from the horse mechanized conceptions of the early 1940's.

In the spring and early summer of this year when the 77th Division was alerted for the Guam operation we had already completed special training and plans for the employment of our reconnaissance troop based on experiences learned by our predecessors in the Central Pacific and in the Southwest Pacific. It had already been foreseen that the division would probably be employed on islands where due to restrictions imposed by terrain, vehicular reconnaissance would be impracticable. And so from the beginning, it was decided to streamline the troop by completely dismounting it, thereby relieving it of much of the equipment with which it was burdened. Then with minor changes in organization the troop was ready to go ashore on any island that might come up in the cards with the old basic mission of getting the information and getting it back.

All vehicles except two 2½ ton and six ¼ ton trucks were eliminated. Along with vehicles went all the .50 caliber machine guns, a number of light machine guns, mortars, bazookas and all the T/E radios. M-1's replaced carbine Seven-man and ten-man rubber boats were added. SCR-193 radios were mounted in the six jeeps and fifteen of the infantry's 300 radios were hand-carried. Personnel were equipped with the infantry combat pack in lieu of the field bag, with sneakers, mechanic's caps, trench knives, grenade carriers, bayonets and extra canteens.

Radios were so distributed as to permit each platoon to have a 300 net, the troop to have both a 193 and a 300 net and the liaison officer to have a 193 as well as a 300 net.

At the same time the troop's T/O had undergone tentative changes. The headquarters platoon was reduced to 44 men with the remainder assigned equally to each reconnaissance platoon. The defense squad, armed with submachine guns, light machine guns and M-1 rifles, was added to the headquarters for the defense of the troop CP. Each reconnaissance platoon now had a total strength of 35 men, eight in the platoon headquarters and nine in each of the three reconnaissance squads. These squads carried a light machine gun and the platoon headquarters carried a 60mm mortar. Some obvious headaches accompanied these tentative changes. However, the mechanics knew they would have their armored cars again some day and the radio operators realized that their job would some time again be more technical than transporting by back a set that any man could operate.

All T/E equipment not required for the operation was turned over to the rear echelon which remained behind. Everything the troop now had could be hand carried except their field ranges and their 193 radios. These were placed on second priority for loading and even they could be left behind or brought up later if it became necessary.

Thus organized and equipped the troop conducted extensive tactical exercises in patrolling and amphibious reconnaissance. The latter training stressed swimming with equipment, handling small boats, estimating tides and currents and studying hydrographic conditions and beach features. Small boat landings were made from destroyers at night and rock landings were practiced until the treachery of coralhead and volcanic rock were no longer considered hazardous. Scouts were swum ashore on lonely strips of beach. Inland patrolling through mountains and jungle against positions established by our own infantry regiments built up stamina, technique and courage. By hard work these men learned that they could land from a surface ship at night in rubber boats, climb over a mountain range, patrol through a jungle and after several days return to their ship with the information they had been sent for. Lessons learned at various amphibious centers and the Jungle Training Center in Hawaii helped these men master hazardous reefs and the problems of living and fighting in the jungle.

With this background the troop felt itself ready for a dawn landing on any man's island, particularly one of Mr. Hirohito's, and on the 24th of July when it came ashore behind infantry elements of the division which were securing the beachhead this troop was a hardened, well-trained outfit anxious to find some Japs and to see what the rest of Guam looked like.

Throughout the entire campaign which lasted for twenty-one days before organized Jap resistance ceased the troop conducted continuous reconnaissance and operated division OP's.

During the beachhead phase of the operation the division was interested in determining the enemy's strength in the south and central part of the island, not only to determine where the Japanese troops were forming for counterattacks but also because future plans called for the division to swing east and northeast across the island on the right of the corps and clean up the north end of the island. This maneuver would not only hit head-on any resistance in the central mountain area but it would also expose the right flank and rear of the division to any Jap forces that might be in the southern half of the island. Although it was believed that the Japs would withdraw to the high ground northeast of Agana, there were still indications as late as 26 July that strong forces were still present in the Facpi Point - Mt. Lamlam - Harmon Road areas. If these Japs were in strength and intended to stay in this area and fight we wanted to know it. On the 27th the reconnaissance troop was given the job of finding out.

This was to be the troop's first contact with the enemy. Up to now not even patrols of the infantry regiments had penetrated more than 1000 to 1500 yards beyond our forward barrage line. Critical points along the southeast and southwest coast were selected and routes thereto covering critical areas in the interior were designated. On the morning of the 27th two patrols set out across the island for objectives on the east coast, two to the southeast and one down the southwest coast. Several days later another patrol was dispatched to reconnoiter to the east coast along the route tentatively chosen for the advance of the division. On the 30th of July another patrol was dispatched to the southeast coast through Talofofo to Port Inarajan. The hidden dangers of the island interior, a chance of being ambushed or cut off by the Japs, and the very newness of the terrain itself combined to make these missions hazardous.

Lt. Simpson's patrol which headed east for Ylig and Pago Bay areas was forced to turn back when the second in command became dangerously ill with dengue and required medical aid. It had gotten half way to its objective. Although the patrol traveled 8,000 yards it encountered no Jap forces.

Lt. Miller's patrol headed east for Talofofo and Ylig Bay. Traveling through the back breaking canebrakes and jungles of the lowlands with climbs to the high ground for observation this patrol successfully evaded the small, nomadic enemy patrols and determined from their movements and from the natives who had escaped from Jap concentration camps that there had been a recent general exodus of all organized units of the enemy to the north. This patrol traveled 24,000 yards and returned on the third day.

The two patrols sent into the thicknesses and cave-pocketed slopes o
Mt. Alifan and Mt. Almagosa had rough sledding from the time they left our
lines until they returned three days later. The slopes of Mt. Almagosa were
ripe with snipers. These patrols were unable to follow there prescribed
routes and had considerable difficulty in maintaining communication with the
troop. They returned after travelling approximately 18,000 yards with information concerning ammunition dumps, Japs in caves and deserted bivouac are;
Although they encountered some Japs their information indicated no organized
enemy in strength.

The patrol sent south along the west coast to Umatac ran into simila:
difficulties of communication. After a three day silence it returned with
about 75 extremely grateful natives but encountered no enemy. It covered
about 21,000 yards in 39 hours.

The patrol reconnoitering the route of advance of the division made
the cross island trek to Pago Bay in about one day. An engineer reconnaissanc
party accompanied this patrol which successfully evaded the enemy except for
one brief encounter which yielded two dead Japs. It covered a total of 13,00(
yards, located Jap troops moving north along the east coast near Pago Bay and
gained valuable information of both the terrain and the enemy.

All of these patrol reports confirmed our estimate that the bulk of
the Jap troops known originally to be in the south-half of the island had
already moved out to the north. This information enabled the division to shi;
its strength to the left, take Mt. Tenjo and to drive straight across the isl;
with record time to the east coast in hot pursuit of the withdrawing Japs with
out too much concern over the vulnerability of an exposed flank.

During the division's attack across the island the troop continued
to patrol on the south flank of the division and when the advance to the nort!
end of the island commenced the troop had the mission of patrolling from the
right flank of the division to the east coast.

While still on the south flank the troop was ordered to reconnoiter
straight across country to Port Inarajan. Lt. Stringer, with part of his
platoon, carried out this mission. They killed two Japs enroute and returned
in three days after covering 28,000 yards in enemy territory. This patrol
covered the areas where our OP's had seen most of the Jap activity in front
of our forward barrage line. The information it gained both from observation
and natives definitely proved that the Japs had withdrawn from this area to
the north.

All of these patrols, the one to Inarajan in particular, contacted
many native Chamorros most of whom were not aware that the Americans had alre;
landed. The excitement and gratification displayed by them as these American
troopers - first white men they had seen since the Japs moved in on December
10, 1941 - appeared from the jungles into the edges of their native clearings
was a moving experience for the men of the patrols. They were showered with
what gifts of value their oppressors had left them. The leaders of patrols
were looked upon as direct emissaries of the government and the local leader
of the native-type underground immediately offered the services of his people
for whatever collaboration might be expected. Life and death decisions concerning the people among the villagers accused of traffic with the Japs were

asked of men of the troop sometimes carrying no more than two stripes. The men and women of the village asked first for arms and organization; then for a chance to even the score with those who had made them bow twice daily to an oppressive, mythical Emperor.

It might be well to mention that friendly native guides who were familiar with the terrain accompanied all of these patrols. It might also be well to mention the problems encountered in coordinating these distant patrols with artillery, air and naval gunfire support. In order not to jeopardize the patrols, it was necessary to have them make periodic reports of their exact positions by radio so that each fire support mission called for could be checked with the location of the patrol before it could be fired. On the other hand, patrols could not be allowed to interfere with defensive fires, particularly those at night in support of front line troops. However, in no case did a fire support request have to be refused on account of these patrols and in one instance a patrol itself was able to direct artillery fire by radio on a small concentration of Jap troops.

During the advance to the north, elements of the troop reconnoitered the area near Yigo where natives reported that the Japs had built a considerable number of concrete tunnels. One platoon surprised ten of the enemy, killing four of these as the rest took to their heels into the jungle. Another mile up the trail disclosed installations, living quarters in caves, CP's that had been thoroughly gone over with artillery fire, an elaborate system of wire communication and an aid station (one live Jap lying in the filth and stench of a dozen of his dead comrades and still showing enough fight to necessitate his elimination) and all the familiar manifestations of what undoubtedly had been the nerve center of a contemplated defensive line.

Proceeding on its mission, the point proved its worth by spotting a machine gun with a crew of four ten yards off the trail in anticipation of the main body. Quick action by the point and a platoon leader accounted for all four of these Japs. Snipers were opening up then from the other side of the trail. Sgt. Johns, one of the platoon sergeants, was carrying a Japanese-English dictionary and a bottle of Scat in the right hand pocket of his fatigue jacket. A sniper found his mark; John grunted, was whirled by the impact and hit the ground. With Scat running down his belly and the corner of the dictionary torn to shreds he was relieved to discover that the round, deflected by the book, had passed through a loose fold in his fatigues without leaving a scratch. When knee mortars started landing up and down the trails, the troop decided that it had something big that called for something bigger. An infantry battalion which followed the reconnaissance troop into this area spent three days cleaning the place out and killed some 350 Japs in so doing.

Up to this point the troop had suffered no battle casualties; however, on the 7th of August a patrol was ambushed along the northeast coast of the island. Its leader, Sgt. Hall, was lost in attempting to outflank and determine the enemy resistance and a member of the patrol was wounded.

Mt. Santa Rosa was secured 9 August and with that came the cessation of all organized enemy resistance in our sector. The right kind of a flag was raised over the entire island of Guam on 10 August. Shortly thereafter the troop returned to the rear with the congratualations of Major General A.D.

Bruce to bollster a C-ration morale and with the right to wear thirteen Bronze Stars written into the records of its members.

This campaign re-emphasized the importance of reconnaissance personnel being thoroughly schooled in the fundamentals of basic training with primary attention to physical conditioning, scouting and patrolling, keen observing and accurate reporting. As one trooper told me a few days after the operation: "It was the things I learned during our first seventeen weeks of basic training that got me through this fight".

FIELD ARTILLERY NOTES

FIRING CHARTS

Firing charts are always a problem to be met with the solution producing the best results. At the initial landing there were available only 1:50,000 maps and lithographs of varying scale, 1:9,000 - 1:12,000 incompletely covering the area. The 1:50,000 map had been previously found too inaccurate for a firing chart. As a consequence, a grid sheet chart was used, tied into the map in its initial coordinates and direction. Target area survey was not performed due to the lack of observation. All fires were observed fires or unobserved fires on previously registered in targets. On D plus 1, photomaps, scale 1:25,000 of various areas were made available in sufficient numbers to be used as a firing chart and by forward observers and liaison parties. The photomaps were accurate enough for an observed firing chart and for short K-transfers unobserved. On arrival on D plus 2, a field artillery battalion with a sufficient quantity of photomaps set up an observed firing chart. One company of an amphibious tank battalion had been assisted in setting up a similar firing chart. Division artillery check points were selected at about 15 yard intervals along the line of advance and all battalions adjusted on them.

S-2 REPORT OF LEYTE OPERATION

1. The artillery information service, supplied a large percentage of the information received by the division, particularly in the form of flash messages that arrived within 5 or 10 minutes of the occurence. The AIS was of particular value to the division during the rapid envelopment movements that led to the seizure of Valencia and the Valencia Airfield, Libangao and Highway #2 - Palompon Road Junction and Palompon. Again it was the sole source of spot information from separate combat patrols and information of troops and supply movement in the enemy's rear areas. The effectiveness of the AIS has been greatly enhanced by the cub airplanes. These were able to report rapidly by radio and pick up and drop messages, information of enemy rear areas and of our troops particularly when they were moving. They were of inestimable value in directing fire on long range targets. To summarize, enemy targets taken under fire by our artillery during the operation are divided into three (3) types: fires in close support of our troops, long range neutralization and harassment fires and counterbattery.

COUNTERBATTERY

Japanese artillery in the operation did at no time develop anywhere near the potential power of artillery. Its use consisted merely in sniping with one or two pieces, using either direct fire or very short ranges,

from positions very close, if not on, the main road. Indirect fire was neither
massed nor fired with precision but rather sprayed on an area with usually up
to 2 rounds fired. Its effect for that reason was merely harassing and
produced negligible damage. This indirect firing generally occurred at dusk.
The number of enemy guns, including infantry close-support guns, employed
against our troops was about forty-eight (48).

REPORT OF AIR LIAISON SECTION, LEYTE OPERATION

Supplies: Aviation 73-octane gasoline must be obtained in the future
operations in order that accidents due to engine failure will be stopped, and
the high rate of engine overhaul will be cut to a minimum. Maximum numbers
of planes must be available at all times during the campaign.

Of the 600 drums of Jap aviation gasoline found in caves, a sample
was tested in a plane. The engine operated perfectly for approximately one (1)
minute then without any backfire or anything else it stopped. After setting
idle for awhile the engine was again started. It operated perfectly. The RPM
was increased to 14 then again it died completely. Increasing and decreasing
the position of the throttle failed to revive the engine. This little experi-
ment might be explained that the neoprene tip on the needle valve of the
carburetor expands upon coming in contact with the Asiatic fuel. At the Field
Artillery School we were told such a condition would happen and to overcome it
the tank should be slushed and a higher needle in place of the neoprene needle
should be used.

CLOSE DEFENSE

All around defense of artillery positions by artillerymen was necessary
to keep down sniper fire and prevent suicide infiltrators from destroying our
pieces with satchel and pole charges at night. This condition required
batteries within battalions to be close together. During the day artillery
patrols reconnoitered and combed close-in areas to clean out snipers. The
medium battalion killed over 6 snipers and night infiltrators by small arms fire.

CLOSE SUPPORT

Forward observers were with all front line companies day and night,
and with large patrols sent out daily on reconnaissance. This provided the
infantry with constant means of obtaining close artillery support. Many of
our observers were worked to the point of exhaustion. At one time six forward
observation parties were sent out from one light battalion. The importance
of forward observers cannot be overemphasized.

At night, all round close support was obtained by moving and turning
batteries for night fires. Fires were adjusted each evening. Night artillery
fires, fired on all, proved effective.

TANK-INFANTRY OPERATION

1. General. Successful joint operation of tanks and infantry depends
upon both elements having an intelligent understanding of the capabilities and
limitations of the other.

Tank personnel must constantly remember that the infantryman is but a human being like himself and wears for protection nothing more formidable than an olive drab shirt. He has good reason to want to avoid the close proximity of tanks during enemy antitank firing.

On the other hand the infantryman must remember that although the tank personnel is protected by formidable armor they will be engaged by every enemy weapon and that their size makes them extremely vulnerable to accurate fire; in addition, there are definite limitations as to the terrain over which the vehicle can maneuver and the fortification which a tank weapon can destroy. The tank needs constant support and cooperation as well as the foot soldier.

2. <u>Basic Principles</u>. The basic principle of fire-and-movement applies to the tank organization as well as the rifle company. Officers responsible for any operation involving both elements should consider the tank as an auxiliary weapon to assist the infantry, but, in turn, should use every available means to make the role of the tank easier. The coordinated use of machine-gun and mortar fire on areas which might hide antitank personnel is particularly desirable. The maneuver of any infantry element or tank will usually weaken some spot of enemy resistance enough to permit additional maneuver by other elements. Cooperation in this manner will inevitably weaken the entire enemy resistance.

3. <u>The Tank Commander</u>. The tank commander automatically becomes a special staff officer to the organization to which he is attached or which he supports. It is his duty to see that positive action of tanks is recommended. There is rarely an area on the battlefield where some tanks cannot be used to advantage. Whatever the number be, whether a single tank or a battalion, they should be used with vigor. The loss of four tanks will rarely result in as many casualties as the annihilation of a single squad.

4. <u>Employment</u>.

a. Tanks either are attached or given the role of direct support. <u>There is only room for one commander in a single zone of action</u>. All weapons in that area must be concentrated to fulfill the mission of the commander.

b. If tanks are attached the commander specifies the battle task to be performed by the tanks after receiving the tank commander's recommendations.

c. When tanks are in support of an infantry organization, the tank commander is informed of the mission and plan of operation of the infantry and the tank commander then uses his tanks forcefully to assist the infantry in every way possible. This is normally done by direct fire support.

d. The decision to attach tanks to infantry or to hold them as direct support weapons depends upon the plan of the higher commander and the personalities of the infantry and tank leaders.

5. <u>Zones of Action</u>.

a. No exact guide can be given as to the number of tanks to be assigned to any particular action. In general the area allotted to tanks should be that which presents the least terrain obstacles but due consideration must be given to the fact that such areas are usually mined. In open country tanks must have room to disperse while greater congestion is permissible in rolling or wooded areas. It is not necessary that a tank be actually in a particular area to be effective there. Ground is covered by fire and a modern tank destroyer or medium tank can destroy antitank weapons for distances well beyond a mile.

b. The area covered by an infantry battalion in open country is usually suitable for one tank company; whereas in rugged country, although more tanks can secure adequate cover there will rarely be an opportunity for more than one platoon to be effective.

6. Cooperation of all Arms.

a. Special emphasis must be placed upon the cooperation and coordination of all arms. It is normal and understandable that an infantry company commander or tank commander should be concerned chiefly with killing the enemy to his direct front from which he is receiving fire. To most effectively accomplish this, the commander will usually get the best results by assisting the troops adjacent to him. The smoke of an infantry mortar can frequently cover the advance of tanks to positions where they will be able to see enemy machine gun nests and other weapons which are delaying the advance. Similarly, tanks will find it profitable to disregard extreme range firing against antitank weapons and concentrate their fire against enemy positions which delay the maneuver of the infantry.

b. The coordinated use of infantry and tanks can only be secured by carefully planned means of control. The tank commander must be able to communicate readily with the infantry commander in his zone of action. Several methods have been experimented on and found successful. Alterations are in progress that will give the tank commander a radio which will permit communication directly with the infantry.

c. Some methods of communication which have been found practicable are:

    (1) Liaison groups with radios follow closely behind the tank commander's tank. Infantry requests are transmitted to the liaison group who pound upon the tank commander's tank with a hammer and pass the message to the turret on a split stick.

    (2) Some infantry radios have been found to operate satisfactorily in tanks and are carried in the commander's vehicle.

    (3) In short, limited-objective operations a telephone has been given to the tank commander and a reel of wire fastened on the rear of the tank so that telephone communication was maintained.

7. Mines.

a. Anti-personnel mines are ineffective against tanks. When such mines are known or suspected consideration should be given to advancing tanks in front of infantry to explode these mines thus clearing a passageway for

- 60 -

infantry who follow in the tank tracks.

b. Antitank mines will put a tank out of action by usually breaking
the tank track but will rarely be strong enough to kill occupants of the tank.
The fact that mines are suspected must not prevent the employment of tanks.
Forceful use of these weapons will inevitably reduce the total loss of lives.
Usually it will be possible to recover the tank during the night following the
operation.

8. Tanks as Troop Carriers. It is entirely feasible to carry infantry
on tanks at the ratio of one infantry platoon to each tank platoon. Every
consideration should be given to this mode of advance. It will frequently be
possible in a situation where the enemy is endeavoring to break off contact.
The advance should be covered by mortar smoke from one position to the next.
The tank turrets will afford almost complete protection against small-arms
fire to the troops thus transported.

9. Tank Positions in the Attack.

a. It is impossible to give any rule to cover the relations of
infantry and tanks in an advance. The question which will usually be upper-
most in the mind of the officer directing such an operation will be whether
to have the tanks precede or follow the infantry. This will vary according
to the information of the enemy and the terrain over which the operation is to
take place. Tanks should precede whenever possible. The enemy are then forced
to disclose their positions in the face of tank operation whereas infantry can
be permitted to advance to positions most suitable to the plan of enemy defense.

b. Tanks will rarely precede an infantry operation at night but may,
under the cover of artillery fire, be moved to advance supporting positions
ready to acheive maximum surprise at dawn.

c. Where attacks are to be made across open ground it is desirable
to dig tank positions well forward during darkness under the cover of friendly
patrols so that when the attack begins tanks may acheive surprise by moving
into such forward supporting positions at dawn or in the early phases of the
attack.

d. Tanks are invulnerable to air-burst artillery and if the plan
of attack permits such operation they should precede the infantry so as to
arrive on the objective while air-burst artillery keeps the enemy in their
positions. Such an operation should be carefully planned so that tanks secure
advantageous positions before artillery ceases fire and are thus ready to use
their machine guns to best advantage when the enemy attempts to man their
weapons.

e. In event the thin-skinned prime movers of infantry antitank weapons
make it impractical for these T/E weapons to perform their combat mission, a
platoon of tank destroyers per battalion should be attached to perform this
vital role. The aggressive spirit of infantry must not be reduced by permitting
them to feel their impotency against enemy armor.

f. Although tanks will frequently find it necessary because of terrain obstacles to move through areas occupied by infantry, it is desirable that tank platoons operate in small groups and thus avoid drawing fire upon the infantry they assist. An example would be a company of tanks operating in a battalion sector. One platoon operating on each flank of the battalion zone of action with the third platoon of the company used as a maneuver force in the rear center would make a practical formation - terrain permitting.

10. Counterattack. Due to the mobility and comparative invulnerability of tanks they are particularly valuable for counterattack. Once an objective is taken immediate reconnaissance should be made to anticipate enemy actions. Tanks may be called upon to move through artillery barrages considerable distances to meet and break up enemy counterattacks during the early stages of such an action. Tanks should not be content to defend on a position but should attack vigorously for this usually affords an opportunity to close with dismounted enemy and should result in heavy enemy casualties.

11. Pursuit.

a. Armor affords the best means of pursuit available to the commander once the enemy's position is broken. Every attempt should be made to prevent the enemy from reforming on new positions and utilizing antitank mines to delay armored action. At nightfall the enemy will endeavor to regroup his forces and to organize strong defensive areas against the next day's advance. In such cases tanks should be used with abandon at dusk. Deep inroads can sometimes be made into the enemy area where enemy resistance is broken by using tank weapons with abandon. The human psychology which causes every individual to feel that weapons are always aimed will result in consternation and near-panic by the fact that large-caliber weapons are behind the enemy lines. If any degree of success is attained friendly infantry can be moved forward on supporting tanks and the "leap-frog" action thus continued throughout the night.

b. Daylight pursuit presents no unusual tactical principles; the rate of advance depends entirely upon the enemy opposition. There is no reason why, under weakening enemy resistance, a tank force as small as a company should not penetrate several miles into enemy territory.

12. Security. Occasionally some infantry is required to furnish security for tank elements. However, when tanks bivouac in rear of friendly infantry the security is automatically afforded. The infantryman is usually far more fatigued than the tank soldier and accordingly the requirements upon him should be the minimum. During darkness tanks may bivouac in close assembly and their only danger is enemy patrols. Dismounted tankmen, with hand grenades and tommy guns, are available in sufficient number to afford the necessary protection. Properly sighted, coaxial tank machine guns, machine guns on ground mounts and antiaircraft .50 caliber weapons present adequate defense if a proper warning system is afforded.

13. Supply. The infantry commander must not disregard the tank commander's problems of supply. Whereas a human being can continue to advance though hungry and fatigued a tank merely stops running when the supply of fuel is exhausted.

WAR DOGS

The following patrol reports indicate the capabilities and limitations of war dogs.

1. <u>Patrol leader of an infantry regiment</u>: - "Earlier reconnaissance had determined the position of a large Japanese bivouac area and after a heavy artillery concentration a combat patrol consisting of thrity-five men, a field artillery forward observer and a scout dog'with handler went into the area. The patrol carried two radios in addition to their individual combat equipment and one day's ration.

"The scout dog and dog trainer took the lead and the patrol made good progress for over three miles into enemy territory. No enemy was sighted before starting on their return trip.

"As the patrol came near a trail junction the dog picked up the scent of the enemy and from his gesture the trainer alerted the patrol. At the junction of the trail the dog indicated a strong scent by his increased alertness and the pull exerted on his leash. These gestures are characteristic of each scout dog and are known thoroughly by his trainer.

"This patrol moved forward with the scout dog in the lead. The dog again indicated a strong scent after several yards further advance. The warning came just in time for the trainer to alert the patrol and the scouts pushed ahead of the dog. Almost immediately twelve (12) armed Japanese appeared directly in front of them. In the fire fight that followed five (5) enemy were killed. The remaining Japanese escaped in the direction from which they had approached.

"The patrol followed the retreating Japanese approximately 200 yards before the dog again indicated the nearness of the enemy. The scouts went forward and upon reaching the crest of a small rise were able to observe and count approximately fifty (50) disorganized Japanese scattering into the dense jungle 200 yards away.

"Actually the dog's actions influenced me to: first, alert the patrol and place the men to an advantage by knowing that the enemy was close at hand thus eliminating the surprise element and giving timely warning for the proper deployment of the patrol; second, advance the patrol rapidly into enemy territory with comparative safety from enemy ambush and sniper fire from the jungle."

2. <u>Sergeant of an infantry regiment</u>: "Recently while on outpost duty, our platoon had the mission of patrolling an area leading to an enemy supply dump. This locality was exceptionally dense because of the thick growth of bamboo, rain forest and scrub, making observation very difficult. For this assignment we had the services of a scout dog and his handler. When the men who were to form this patrol were briefed before leaving the capabilities of the dog were thoroughly explained to them.

"Shortly after starting on our mission the dog, by his actions, indicated the possibility of enemy being present in a heavily wooded thicket to the left of the trail we were travelling. A small detachment was sent forward to investigate the area and found eight packs fully loaded with food and clothing which the enemy had concealed. Continuing on our mission, about ten or twelve feeder trails were encountered and at each of the trails the dog's reactions were negative. As a counter-check, small groups were dispatched down each trail for a distance of approximately 300 yards. In every case they found nothing to warrant further investigation nor were there any indications of the enemy having used these trails recently.

"Proceeding on the main trail the dog again showed interest at something to our left. Here, more packs and equipment were found but the enemy had evacuated the area. Soon afterwards our destination was reached a distance of approximately one and one-half miles being covered.

"I believe this patrol moved faster than it ordinarily would because of the use of the dog. On our return every member of the patrol was enthusiastic about the use of scout dogs for this particular type of work. It is recommended that more of the dogs be secured if possible so that they can be used more extensively. Training of patrols with the dogs would increase the efficiency of the team. It was clearly evident that the use of dogs on patrols bolsters the confidence of each man and helps remove the uneasiness and tension that naturally is present in a mission of this kind. It also enables patrols to cover more ground in less time since the danger of ambush is removed."

3. Second Lieutenant of an infantry regiment: - "My platoon was designated for a patrol with the mission of finding a main trail leading north, checking the area for evidence of the enemy, kill as many as possible and then to withdraw to safety. The patrol consisted of one officer, two non-commissioned officers and twenty-three enlisted men armed with one BAR, one tommy-gun and twenty-four rifles. We were given one scout dog and trainer to assist the patrol. The weather was fair although it had rained the previous night and the ground was still muddy. The terrain was hilly and covered by dense undergrowth.

"The patrol at one time was alerted by the dog and immediately searched the trail and both flanks. This search resulted in the discovery that the area to which the dog was pointing had recently been occupied by the enemy.

"On another occasion the dog halted the patrol and the trainer called me forward and explained that from the dog's actions there were, or had been, a large group of persons in the area to our left front. I sent one squad to make a check and to report on what was there. Upon returning from the reconnaissance the squad leader reported another American patrol had been seen on a trail two hundred yards away.

"A scout dog is of great assistance on a patrol as he relieves the tension that the men generally have. Also the dog is a time saver. We covered twice the distance with the dog that we would have covered alone. It was evident that the dog became alert by the scent of our own patrols as well as the enemy. However, this in no way distracts from his usefulness."

4. **Sergeant of an infantry regiment:** - "A reconnaissance patrol consisting of fifteen men from the intelligence and reconnaissance platoon was given the mission of locating an enemy bivouac area thought to be a few thousand yards to the north of our defensive positions. One scout dog and trainer was obtained to accompany the patrol. The patrol left the outposts at 0845 hours and returned at 1500 hours the following day. Rain fell heavily throughout the patrol.

"In moving up the trail which was followed for the first portion of the journey it was found that the dog and trainer, in the lead, forced the patrol to move at a slower pace than they normally would have. After moving a few hundred yards along the trail the patrol took a cross-country route through the rain forest.

"Once in the rain forest the dog and trainer at the head of the column slowed down the progress of the patrol even more than before. The terrain in this area varied from slightly rolling to hilly. The ground consisted of rough coral with many crevices. In addition to the rain forest trees there was great difficulty in negotiating the dog through this terrain. The leash became tangled in vines at frequent intervals. Also the dog did not always proceed in the direction which the trainer intended and it was necessary to pull him back and head him in the right direction. All of this made the movement of the patrol very slow.

"Several times during the first day of the trip the trainer stated that the dog had scented someone to the front. The patrol stopped each time that this happened in order to investigate. In one of these cases it was found that Japanese might have been present at the time the dog gave the signal, but in the other cases no trace of Japanese was found.

"During the night while the patrol was in bivouac the dog behaved very well. He made no excessive noise.

"When the patrol started back on the second day, the dog was placed at the rear of the column so that it would be possible for the patrol to move faster. The dog was of no value as a scout in this position but the terrain over which the patrol travelled in returning had been partially reconnoitered on the previous day and was considered to be safe.

"It is my opinion that scout dogs could be used with excellent results when moving along trails in the jungle. They might be used satisfactorily on a cross-country patrol if the vegetation were easy to get through. On a cross-country patrol through thick vegetation I should say that they could not be used to good advantage. In the latter case the dog and trainer moving at the head of the column impedes the progress of the patrol greatly and in making their way through the brush cause quite a bit of extra noise."

5. **Sergeant of an infantry regiment:** - "I was a member of a short range combat patrol assigned the mission of seeking and destroying any enemy troops that could disrupt our lines of communications. The patrol consisted of a rifle platoon (31 men), section of heavy machine guns (17 men) and a section of 81mm mortars (17 men). The patrol formation was as follows: In the lead was the scout dog and trainer, followed by two rifle squads, messenger dog and trainer, heavy machine gun section and another rifle squad bringing up

the rear - the 81mm mortars being left in a rear area to give immediate supporting fire if needed.

"The terrain was a series of steep ridges approximately 100 yards high, covered with coral rock and heavily jungled with the exception of the top of the ridges. The day was cloudy and visibility fair.

"The patrol had been on the march about an hour when the scout dog indicated the presence of the enemy. With this information the patrol leaders moved two rifle squads on a line and advanced towards the enemy area. At this time communications were disrupted to the rear and the messenger dog was sent back to the weapons section with orders for the section to go into position and cover the advance of the rifle troops. The patrol, on advancing to the enemy position, found that it had been recently evacuated. The remainder of the journey was covered without incident.

"During this mission, the scout dogs were an excellent preventative against possible enemy ambushes. The timely warning by the scout dog enabled the patrol to take up an offensive position prior to contact with the enemy. When no other means of communication is available the messenger dog can be used to take messages throughout the unit and thereby insure constant means of communication."

6. <u>Sergeant of an infantry regiment:</u> - "I was in command of a short range reconnaissance patrol to seek out enemy troops who might have been in close proximity to our perimeter.

"Eight men armed with three thompson sub-machine guns, one BAR and four riflemen, plus two dog trainers and one scout and one messenger dog (one dog trainer remained to receive messages) comprised the patrol.

"Terrain was fairly level, coral rock, moderately jungled with ridges to each flank paralleling route of patrol. Rain was falling heavily throughout the patrol. Visibility was fair.

"When alerted by the dog the trainer reported enemy had been scented on a slight slope to left front. BAR man, one tommy-gunner and two riflemen moved to the area in which enemy was reported but found nothing. This was duplicated several times but each was a false alarm. In each case the patrol dispersed off the trail and a group was dispatched to scented area.

"When dead enemy were passed, the dog did not stop to sniff or look at the bodies. The dogs urinated too often causing the patrol to pause and giving a sniper a clean shot at the lead dog or members of the patrol. The dogs also moved with bursts of speed which caused the patrol to over extend and then crowd alternately. Upon returning to our perimeter the dog paid no attention to our outposts. The messenger dog was not used.

"If dogs had received prior training with infantry patrols and dog trainers were more thoroughly indoctrinated with scouting and patrolling the dogs should prove successful. No doubt in jungle, where visibility is limited, the dog's ability to smell an enemy is advantageous but the dogs hardly proved advantageous on this patrol."

7. **S-3 of an infantry battalion:** - "Dogs have been used only for small reconnaissance patrols by this battalion and no enemy has been encountered on any of these patrols. The dogs led out well on these patrols and traveled very quietly. However, we have used them to hunt out our own outposts in practice patrols and found that they do an excellent job of locating an outpost well before it can be located by accompanying scouts. This was on a clear day, through thick brush and the dog was used in front of the point of the patrol.

"The dog is a definite aid to this kind of patrolling and should be very valuable in locating enemy outposts or hunting out stragglers after the main resistance has been broken."

8. **Second lieutenant of an infantry regiment:** - "Two dogs, one scout and one messenger, accompanied us on a three-day patrol. The messenger dog was not used because of the distance covered but I believe in short patrols through hilly country where radio is not reliable the dog would be very useful. The scout dog was used only part of the time because he seemed to tire fast and thus hold back the patrol. I do not believe that dogs should be used on long patrols unless used in pairs that could alternate as scout at hourly intervals."

9. All units recommend that the mission and available enemy information be thoroughly explained to the dog handler before the patrol sets out. Likewise the patrol should be thoroughly informed as to the limitations and habits of the dog and the rules the trainer must enforce in order to get maximum efficiency from the animal.

10. It is interesting to note that Reports 4 and 6, both of which reported unfavorably on the dogs, state that rain was falling continuously throughout the patrols. This factor may or may not have had a bearing on the performance of the dog. There are also indications that the same dog was used for both patrols although this cannot be conclusively proved. It is known that one infantry regiment borrowed one scout dog from another infantry battalion and that later one scout dog from the battalion was evacuated because he made excessive noise on patrol.

11. **Patrol leader of an infantry regiment:** - "A patrol consisting of four officers and one rifle platoon supported by one litter team, one scout dog and two native guides left the battalion command post. A lieutenant was in charge.

"For the first thousand yards we attempted to use the dog with two natives and two scouts in front of him. However, the dog trainer asked to be moved ahead of the scouts and from that point the dog and trainer occupied the position of lead scout.

"The dog alerted the patrol at four different times during the movement out. The first time was on our approach to our own roadblock and the dog alerted approximately one hundred yards before we got to it.

"At the occasion of the second alert the dog was held back while scouts from the rifle platoon went ahead to scout out the area ahead. The scouts worked forward about one hundred and fifty yards when they found an enemy bivouac estimated to have been used two days before but at the time un-occupied. We passed through the bivouac and the dog alerted again on approach of two dead enemy.

"At the time of the final alert eight enemy were discovered approxi-mately forty-five yards from the lead scouts.

"In my opinion the dogs are very valuable on patrols into unknown territory. Their alert usually comes long before the scouts could detect any presence. However, I would recommend that after alerting the patrol the dog should be moved back into the patrol while the rifle scouts make a detailed reconnaissance of the area. The dogs are too valuable to risk keeping forward after the initial alert."

12. Second lieutenant of an infantry regiment: - "Ours was a three day patrol with mission of scouting Japanese positions. The patrol consisted of two officers, two dog handlers, four enlisted men, three police boys and nine native carriers; number of dogs, two (2).

"Dogs were used on the trails in the rear of, and to supplement, two scouts. Dogs "alerted" upon approaching any unusual object on or near the trail such as bivouacs, huts, villages, etc. Dogs "alerted" at a distance of from thirty to sixty yards from object. Several times dogs "alerted" and no reason for the alert was found by scouts. When operating two to three hundred yards from Japanese positions in the area north of a little town, the dogs were in constant alert. Scouts in front of the dog did not seem to interfere with his ability to detect foreign objects. In one instance a dog was taken to an observation post located less than forty yards from four Japanese. This distance was across a stream. The wind apparently did not favor the dog and he failed to "alert" at any time although he was kept in the observation post for about an hour.

"At night when the patrol was bivouacked in an area known to be less than five hundred yards from the enemy the dogs were posted at each end of the area for security. This seemed to ease the members of the patrol and instill confidence in the security in them. One dog was obviously "spoiled" and whined when tied at a distance of less than five yards from his master. The dog had to be moved from his security position to quiet him and allow his master to remain under cover.

"It was found that dogs had no trouble in traversing steep terrain which was very difficult for the patrol members. Dogs had a tendency to move faster than scouts could be expected to thoroughly cover this area.

"Dogs are handicapped in open terrain as their vision is poor and they depend almost entirely upon the sense of smell. It is believed that scouts should be moved forward in such terrain and the dogs disregarded. If the wind is not favorable (from the head) dogs should not be used.

"It is believed that dogs are excellent for night security. The greatest advantage is that using dogs eases the men.

"The frequent "alerting" of dogs on patrol tends to make the members of the patrol uneasy until they are accustomed to it.

"It is believed that dogs are valuable on patrol only when supplemented by expert scouting by scouts, trained to recognize signs in the dog's (each dog differs) behavior and use these as a guide in scout action. It is not believed that dogs and handlers should be used as a substitute for scouts."

13. Captain of an infantry regiment: - "A forty man patrol left the forward command post with a mission of cutting enemy wire communications and to establish ambushes on a trail. Four scout dogs from a war dog platoon were attached for this mission. The remainder of this report deals only with the workings of these dogs as follows:

"During route, these dogs alerted several times but upon extensive patrolling in vicinity nothing was found. On one of the mornings at about 0900 hours the dogs alerted again and a very large old Japanese bivouac area was found. That same afternoon a small reconnaissance party of six men was sent north along the trail. After travelling some 200 yards the scout dogs alerted. The sergeant in charge of the patrol moved up to the dog and raised his rifle to his shoulder. In just a few seconds a Nip came over the hill about forty yards to front of patrol. The lead Japanese was killed. The following day at about 0830 hours another security patrol of approximately six men were sent south on the trail. After traveling about 200 yards the dog alerted but because the sergeant in command of the patrol was in front of the dog he was not warned and ran into a Japanese ambush. The remainder of the patrol were alerted and for this reason only one man was wounded and three of the enemy were killed. Immediately following this action the entire forty-man patrol returned to the battalion command post.

"The idea of all patrol members is that these dogs are of a great value. The lead scouts have great confidence in their knowledge that the dog's instincts are far more acute than their own.

"One thing that was brought to my attention is that on a long patrol with heavy equipment a scout gets just as fatigued as the rest and the more tired he becomes the less alert he is. The dogs will hardly ever become tired on the type of patrolling we are doing and seem never to relax their alertness."

14. Second lieutenant of an infantry regiment: - "A patrol of fifty men twenty-five native carriers and police boys, two dogs and two handlers left the battalion command post at 0930 hours and returned at 1600 hours two days later covering the area from the command post to the nearby river.

"Factual description and accomplishments: Since we had native scouts and guides we did not rely much on the dogs. We did find them of value as security during night bivouacs. I used the dogs as the leading scouting element all the way back but we encountered no enemy so I cannot give information as to value of the dogs in action against the Japanese. I did have the opportunity of watching them work in enemy territory and have arrived at certain personal conclusions.

"On two separate occasions the dogs alerted us to the fact that we were within the immediate vicinity of strangers. Both times we discovered natives coming toward us some sixty yards up the trail. Although the dogs alerted at any strange smell or sound I did not find that the use of dogs slowed up our movement much.

"Value of Dogs on patrol: Dogs cannot take the place of native scouts and guides and their use is limited but they do have possible uses. In close jungle where fields of fire are limited, I believe that dogs, because of their acute sense of smell and hearing, can ordinarily detect the presence of Japanese and prevent walking into an ambush. The only time we encountered natives the dogs detected them at least sixty yards away. Dogs would be of little value in open terrain. They are of distinct value as security during night bivouacs."

15. Captain of an infantry battalion: - "During the recent operations of this battalion for a period of eleven days, we had at our disposal several war dogs. We used the war dogs (scout) on several different patrols which included reconnaissance, combat and trail blocks. The patrol leaders of two different three day patrols reported that the scout war dog was very helpful. Both patrols were alerted by the dogs in plenty of time to enable them to have the upper hand with the enemy and in both cases Japanese soldiers were killed. Talking with the lead scouts of our infantry patrols the individual scout reports that he feels much more confident when operating with dogs. They state that the dogs keen sense of hearing and smelling saves the patrols from enemy ambushes.

"The scout war dogs were also used on trail blocks and were found very helpful as they did not sleep soundly and were very easily alerted. The dogs are well trained and did not bark or make any noise that would give the enemy warning of our positions.

"The only draw back on the dogs that we could find by talking to our patrol leaders was that while trying to make time the dogs would alert the patrol leaders when coming to old Japanese bivouac areas or enemy equipment. On several occasions the dogs alerted the patrol and the patrol leader immediately dispersed his patrol to engage in a fire fight and found later that the dog had alerted on an old time bivouac area. I do not believe this could be considered a draw back for caution saves lives and time saved cannot be compared with lives saved.

"This battalion would like more training with scout dogs and patrol leaders in our recent patrolling state that they would like to have scout war dogs to use on all patrols in enemy territory."

16. Lieutenant Colonel of an infantry regiment: - "I am convinced that the war dogs have a definite place for practical employment in the infantry combat team. I have observed their practical employment in training and in combat. I feel that they have a definite use for the purpose for which they are trained.

"Scout dogs alerted a patrol of impending danger and in sufficient time for the patrol to clear the trail and prepare for trouble.

"When the patrols set up a perimeter for the night the scout dogs gave the men of the patrol greater confidence and hence permitted a more restful night for all concerned.

"On one occasion when the wind was blowing in the direction of a marsh near a creek bed the scout dog was unaware of the presence of the Japanese, whereas the native scouts and police boys had already alerted the patrol of the danger. The messenger dogs do not function well when the distance between the sender and receiver is over two miles.

"The dog handlers are competent is so far as handling the dogs are concerned but they need more training in basic subjects and junglecraft."

17. Colonel of an infantry regiment: -

    a. (1) "Scout dogs have been attached for several months. Prior to their attachment to this unit, the scout dogs were used on local security patrols and as sentinels within the perimeter.

        (2) These security patrols, consisting of one (1) officer and six (6) men plus one dog and handler, covered the area in the vicinity of the road block for approximately seven hundred (700) yards in all directions.

        (3) Although no contact was made with the enemy the dogs did discover our own patrols and outpost at distances of sixty (60) to seventy (70) yards. They were valuable in picking up scents and guiding the men to the areas that had been previously occupied in addition to following tracks several days old.

    b. "Two reconnaissance patrols were dispatched; one commanded by a 1st lieutenant with sixteen (16) men and two (2) dogs and the other commanded by a 2nd lieutenant with twelve (12) men and one (1) dog. Both patrols were of forty-eight (48) hours duration and both had the mission of reaching and investigating a village and all trails between there and the road block. The 1st lieutenant and his patrol went north and east while the 2nd lieutenant led his patrol due east.

    c. (1) The terrain traversed by the 1st lieutenant and his patrol was extremely rugged with no trails and each dog was relieved from the lead position by the other dog every hour although the men tired before the dogs.

        (2) "A dog, when alerted by a noise, stops and scents. If negative he proceeds along the original route but if he detects anything he heads in the direction from which alerted

        (3) "A dog is alerted from a greater distance going upstream than going down.

(4) "A dog when in the lead of our troops cannot detect anything to the rear. He can detect anything to the front a hundred (100) yards and more if the wind is right and if there is no hill between him and the quarry.

(5) "When a fire fight is in progress, the dog, if on a leash, lies down, remains quiet and does not get excited.

d. Reaction at night: —

(1) "The dog at night sleeps with his leash around his handlers wrist. He alerts at the slightest sound and if the handler does not awaken he will whimper to attact his attention.

(2) "They remain very quiet in bivouac and will not bark. The barking of wild dogs does not effect the scout dogs.

(3) "They were very useful as perimeter guards as they pick up the slightest movement.

e. (1) "The use of dogs enables patrols to move faster as they cover both sides of the trail and help in preventing an ambush.

(2) "The men have extreme confidence in the ability of the dogs".

18. First lieutenant of a cavalry reconnaissance troop: — a. "Entire performance of dogs and trainers was excellent.

b. "On the march to the position assigned, about 7000 yards, over most difficult terrain and jungles, the dogs were alert and aggressive at all times. At 2010 one night the dogs on the right road block alerted to the approach of two Japs, faintly discernible, who subsequently withdrew. At least three times during the following two days the dogs alerted to the approach of the enemy, one time of which actual contact and observations were accomplished.

c. "As far as I know, the dogs did not fail to alert upon contact. An interesting fact was that in the rain, though sound was subdued, the dogs operated with even more acute smell. However, they are handicapped when in a deep ravine before crossing a stream and moving up a steep hill and have difficulty detecting any presence of enemy on the top. This was the only disadvantage I found. After three days exposure one dog caught a mild cold and probably was not able to be entirely depended upon. He subsequently recovered and on the last day and the return march was operating normally.

d. "The two trainers were excellent. They were aggressive, cooperative and had amazing control and obedience over their dogs.

e. "I felt a great deal of confidence in the dogs and believe that when possible they can be used to a great advantage at all times."

19. Conclusions:

As a result of the tests described above it is believed that the following conclusions are justified:

a. War dogs are of material assistance to the success of operations conducted in jungle terrain.

b. War dogs will give warning of enemy presence within thirty yards under most conditions and greater distances under favorable circumstances. Warnings thus given will prevent ambush of friendly patrols and, in addition, enable patrol leaders to plan attacks prior to their presence being discovered by the enemy.

c. Security provided by war dogs enables patrols to advance at a greatly increased rate of speed along jungle trails allowing more area to be covered in a given time.

d. Presence of war dogs operates to increase the confidence of patrols as a whole.

e. War dogs tire easily and need frequent rests when accompanying patrols in thick country. The health of the dogs working in tropic climate and difficult terrain has been good. The scout dog never relaxes his alertness despite the hardships of difficult terrain and long distances traversed by the patrol.

f. The scout dog proved to be an efficient, reliable and excellent sentinel at prepared trail blocks and in perimeter defensive positions due to the dog's ability to detect the faintest sound. In this regard, night infiltration by the enemy can be detected by use of dogs with sentinels.

g. The use of scout dogs in perimeter defense gives the men a feeling of security and permits them to get more rest and sleep.

h. Messenger dogs have limited value in jungle warfare. The messenger dog worked efficiently on short patrols. His employment on long patrols is of doubtful value.

REPORT ON MAPS AND PHOTOMAPS USED DURING AN AMPHIBIOUS OPERATION

The following is submitted:

a. Subject of Report: Maps and Photomaps used by an infantry division during the operation.

b. Purpose of the Report: To ascertain the requirements, use, correctness of size, scale, color and interpretations of the maps with the view of increasing the usefulness of this organization in map making for future operations.

c. Outline.

SECTION I

At the request of the amphibious force, I was assigned to G-2 of an infantry division to act as forward G-2 observer. My duties were intelligence work in general and especially to observe the usefulness of the present maps, their correctness as to scale, vegetation, coral reefs, planimetric detail, interpretations and grid. As a representative of the unit that prepared the basic maps for the operation and with my mission in mind, I questioned company commanders, platoon leaders, enlisted men of the assault groups, naval personnel, higher echelon commanders and artillery commanders and personnel both before landing, during the landing and at the front lines. The comments and suggestions given me together with my own observations are listed below under the heading of the various types of maps used.

SECTION II

Planning Maps:

The planimetric maps were, in general, very good. These maps at a scale of 1/20,000 were used as basic maps from which all other maps were made. The 1/3,000 maps were portions of the 1/20,000 maps blown up photographically and were annotated with additional interpretations, plans for the various phases, beaches, sector lines and firing areas. The vegetation shown on these maps was good although a possible additional symbol of areas which contain cocoanuts and heavy brush together might be advantageous. The present interpretation of the coral leaves a great deal to be desired but until methods of actually determining the hydrographic conditions surrounding the coral heads and beaches are available the present method cannot be improvised. Most comment on this feature was favorable in the extreme. The colors used on the maps met a favorable reception. The grid squares themselves were numbered rather than the grid lines and this fact seemed to confuse the using troops. It is recommended that this be changed on future maps. In addition, grid numbers reading "right" could be in one color and grid numbers reading "up" could be printed in another color. It is thought that this will help prevent reading wrong coordinates by the using troops. Some unfavorable comment was received as to the size of the 1/3,000 maps. This large map size was extremely useful in study, planning and briefing troops as to their missions but was too large for effective use by squads during actual combat. An adequate supply of planimetric maps were made available to the troops.

SECTION III

Photo Maps:

The 1/20,000 photomaps used during the operations were controlled by the basic 1/20,000 planimetric maps. Both S-2 and S-3 of division artillery reported that the photomaps were very accurate in distance and direction.

These maps were used exclusively for firing and after a few corrections were applied the firing became very accurate. No unfavorable comment was heard in regard to these maps. An adequate supply was available to the troops.

SECTION IV

Aerial Photographs and relief maps (Models):

The stereo pairs and single aerial photographs furnished were essential to study and planning by higher commanders. The few low obliques were also of incalculable value. It is recommended however that stereo pairs, single photographs and low obliques be furnished, if possible, in larger quantities so that platoon commanders and NCO's have them available for study.

The relief maps (Models) were very accurate in their representation of planimetric details. They afforded the infantrymen an exact picture of the ground and enabled him to study in advance the terrain he was to fight on. The colors were vivid and helped to make more understandable the type of terrain to be encountered. It was suggested that an enlarged relief map of each particular beach to be landed upon by the assault troops would be helpful.

SECTION V

Conclusions:

1. In general, no unfavorable comments were received concerning the maps. Vegetation, coral, scale, grid and interpretation were presented adequately and as completely as possible under present circumstances.

2. The photomaps were more than sufficiently accurate for use by artillery.

3. The relief maps (Models) were of immeasurable value for study by the troops.

4. Colors used in the various types of maps were very good.

5. An adequate number of maps were made available to troops.

6. Further study of ground conditions by qualified observers during future operations would undoubtedly be advantageous to the unit making the maps.

SECTION VI

Recommendations:

1. That an additional symbol for cocoanuts with brush be attempted.

2. That facilities be made for additional study and comparison of coral as it appears on the photos and as it is actually on the ground. This may be accomplished in part by observers during future operations.

3. That grid lines be numbered rather than grid squares and that the west-east coordinates be printed in a different color from the south-north coordinates.

4. That maps printed for use of units in actual combat do not exceed 21" x 28".

5. That relief maps (Models) be provided for transports in the following numbers: one model when the trip is over 7 days in length and 2 models when the trip is less than 7 days in length.

6. That larger relief maps of assault beaches be prepared.

7. That three-way liaison be made between the requesting agency, the air unit performing the photo mission and the mapping unit preparing the map.

8. That all maps of any kind used in an operation be made from one basic map so that differences in mapping technique and interpretation will not confuse the using troops.

9. That the mapping unit be consulted as to the feasibility of any mapping project before the requesting agency makes formal request.

10. It is strongly recommended that at least one officer from the mapping unit be sent as an observer on all future operations. This will enable the mapping unit to be kept abreast of mapping needs and will insure that officers become better experienced and qualified to perform their duties.

STAFF INSPECTION OF CONSTRUCTION ACTIVITIES

1. Observations on recent inspections have indicated that certain construction deficiencies exist which have not been observed nor corrected during inspections made of such construction by higher staff representatives having technical supervision over such activities.

2. It is desirable that the principal features which should be covered in such inspections be defined in order to insure that consideration is given by the appropriate technical staffs to the principal factors affecting efficient prosecution of such construction operations under their supervisory control. Unless specific objectives and points for consideration are listed and specifically assigned to and covered by the inspecting officers during the inspection the inspection may be haphazard and omit major deficiencies.

3. The following notes are furnished covering items that should be checked into on such inspections:

a. Supervisory Staff: Check should be made that the engineer supervisory staff is adequate and qualified for the supervision of the work. If this staff is inadequate or unsuited the entire construction operation will be inefficient. This staff must be qualified to analyze the overall project; to determine the requirements of the job in hand; to initiate and supervise the necessary engineer reconnaissance; to determine and analyze the resources available; to plan and lay out the work, including the most efficient execution. A deficiency in staff, even though representing an insignificant percentage of the overall engineering force, may result in a major percentage deficiency in the execution of the entire project. High priority should be given to the movement of such staff personnel in the earliest phases of task force operations.

b. Engineer Reconnaissance: Check should be made that early and extensive provisions have been made for engineer reconnaissance to include within the limitations of time and forces available a survey of the work involved; determination of the most suitable areas and sites for required construction; a determination of the most difficult areas or features of work; a thorough and complete reconnaissance of quantity and suitability of locally available construction materials, such as timber, coral, sand and gravel, etc., including the relative efforts required for securing these materials and transporting them to the various areas where they are required. On many projects observed, this engineer reconnaissance has been inadequate. Unless the basic data of features of work and sources of suitable materials are made available in the earliest stages of construction, the project cannot be efficiently planned nor executed.

c. Planning, Layout and Supervision: It is essential that the project be efficiently planned and laid out. A quick staff study of several potential layouts of roads, dromes, etc., made on paper can effect savings of many thousands of cubic yards of grading and in useless expenditure of manpower and plant which would otherwise be required on inefficiently or inadequately planned and laid out construction. Check should therefore be made that plans and layouts have been reduced to paper and not merely in the minds of those who propose generally to execute an overall construction project. Check should also be made that graphic progress schedules have been prepared, indicating the break-down of the project into its important sub-features covering the calendar schedules over which these various features are to be undertaken with actual progress attained also indicated thereon as work proceeds. The preparation and maintenance of such progress schedules will insure well in advance a means of control that forces and plant are adequately distributed to the various features of work, and also provide an additional visual check as to the periods at which critical construction materials are required. Having in mind the delays which prevail in securing supplies and transportation for supplies, it is obvious that these requirements must be foreseen well in advance if construction is not to be intermittently delayed due to shortage or lack of materials.

d. Supervision: It is essential that the local staffs, by continuing personal inspection and by receipt, review and analysis of operational reports, check that the work is being efficiently executed. This supervision includes also the observation and supervision of subordinate unit headquarters and of officers and men executing subordinate phases of the work. It includes in the preliminary phases, over the periods prior to the operation and the execution of the work, technical supervision of the training of officers and men within their units to insure that they are qualified to lay out, supervise and execute work, operate and maintain plant and are instructed in the fundamentals of all basic military construction. It is apparent that on certain staffs and in many units the degree of training can and should be materially improved.

e. Drainage: The importance of adequate drainage cannot be over-stressed. On every inspection, careful check should be made to insure that suitable provisions have been made in the earliest stages of construction for adequate drainage. It is an elemental and basic phase of all construction operations the importance of which is not sufficiently appreciated. Drainage measures net major dividends for the amount of work expended in reducing the overall work required.

f. Choice of Materials: On many projects, difficulties have resulted from the use of faulty materials for airdrome construction, road work, etc. These deficiencies have occurred on projects where many representatives of various staffs have inspected the project during its construction but apparently failed to observe the materials employed or the test measures taken to determine their relative suitability.

g. Construction Methods: Check should be made by inspecting representatives of the construction methods employed on the specific project. In many cases an unbalanced effort will be found, such as a deficiency in excavating capacity and a surplus in truck or materials hauling capacity in one area and an inverse ratio of these features in another. Check should be made as to whether the materials being emplaced in various sections of the project are being procured from the nearest source of suitable materials. Check should be made of the balancing of construction capacity as represented by units and plant commensurate with the relative difficulty or requirement of the specific features of work. Consideration should be given to what items of special plant should be provided or supplemented to the construction force to increase output. General check should be made that the construction methods being employed are such as to insure maximum efficiency and speed of construction.

h. Bottleneck: It will generally be found that some feature, such as excavating capacity, dump truck transport capacity, accessibility to suitable materials as controlled by bridge construction or some similar feature is the control on the entire project. Special measures should be taken to determine what is the controlling factor and what steps can be taken to remedy it and provide sufficient concentration of effort on the controlling feature so as to correct it promptly.

i. Construction Equipment: Special check should be made on the adequacy and balancing of equipment to do the work required and, in particular, on the provisions made for the maintenance of that equipment. It must be especially appreciated that equipment on the site and on the work is immeasurably more valuable than similar equipment back in the United States or in rear depots. It is far more important that the equipment on the site be kept in operating condition over the greatest possible time than merely to have a paper credit for such equipment in rear areas. Check should therefore be made that suitable measures have been taken for the servicing of this equipment; that an adequate stock of fast moving spare parts is available at the site to reduce non-operating periods to the minimum; that an adequate maintenance crew of mechanics is available to effect necessary repairs; and that the supply procedure for the procurement of necessary spare parts to effect repairs is established and understood, including the procedure for authorization for air shipment priority, where warranted of critical parts not available. In connection with preliminary measures for such operations, unit staffs and commanders should insure that adequately trained operators and mechanics are provided in their units; and where not, that suitable numbers are trained in the various schools set up for that purpose.

j. Training: Check should be made that officers and men are sufficiently trained to execute the work in hand and, in particular, that they have knowledge of and access to appropriate training and technical references affecting such construction. It is too late after construction is started to train the units for the immediate work in hand. It is therefore essential that continuing inspection of units be made to insure that officers and men are adequately trained for the execution of the type of construction they will be called upon to perform. These inspections should insure that these units are familiar with such references as pertain to construction methods of airdromes, roads, bridges, etc; that the personnel charged with maintenance of plant are acquainted with the training references pertaining to plant and plant maintenance and in particular, that officers and men secure actual training and experience on such work. Check should therefore be made by the various staffs of the training measures employed in the various units, to include unit schools and special schools which should be established to insure that this training is adequately provided.

4. It is to be stressed that our objective is not merely that our engineer units and plant be engaged on a frantic all-out effort. That may gain the commendation and respect of other commanders and branches who observe the tremendous amount of engineer activity underway. Our real objective should insure that, by efficient planning supervision and coordination by the responsible engineer headquarters, the maximum of results will be attained most quickly by the minimum of overall engineer effort. There are not enough engineer means available to do all that should be done within the target dates desired. In order to attain that objective it is incumbent on all engineer staffs to insure that the essential planning and supervision are of the highest order.

5. Only by continuing inspections, seeking and analyzing the foregoing problems and potential deficiencies, with efficiency of our engineer units in their allotted tasks be secured and our important engineer mission successfully performed.

THE FOLLOWING COMMENTS ARE STATEMENTS OF OVERSEAS OBSERVERS ON CWS MATTERS

1. One observer mentions that reliable visual ground-air communications, probably by use of colored smokes, should be made available.

    Comment: Colored smoke grenades, suitable for this use, are now available.

2. One report stresses the requirement for an American pack howitzer.

    Comment: Attention is invited to the fact that in jungle warfare the 4.2" chemical mortar is a satisfactory substitute for the pack howitzer.

3.   One observer calls for the use of forward observers for mortars.

   Comment: Fire control personnel of chemical mortar battalions are
              trained in the duties of forward observers.

4.   One report mentions the requirement of a delay fuze for mortar shell.

   Comment: Such a delay fuze is now available for use with 4.2" HE
              and WP shell.

5.   One observer notes that correct estimation of avenues of approach
enabled a mortar unit to inflict a great number of casualties using HE.

   Comment: This is applicable to the 4.2" chemical mortar, firing
              HE and WP.

6. a.   One observer mentions the need for a light mask in the jungle.
Troops will not carry the heavy service mask.

       Comment: This suggests that a plan be drawn whereby the mask
                  will be kept in forward area storage ready for distri-
                  bution in minimum time if, when, and as indicated.

    b.   Masks for use in jungle warfare must be waterproofed.

7. a.   The flame thrower is mentioned.

       Comment: The flame thrower is a good weapon of opportunity.
                  Men who use the flame thrower must be thoroughly train-
                  ed. Units that conduct flame thrower operations must
                  have trained assault teams and these teams must be
                  given the maximum possible artillery, mortar and small
                  arms support by the units available, including the
                  use of smoke and HE to isolate their target from
                  other field fortifications in the enemy's organized
                  position.

    b.   Failure of flame throwers is noted.

       Comment: The new cartridge ignition for M2-2 portable flame
                  throwers insures ignition. The mechanized flame thrower
                  has been developed so that it is sure to ignite
                  provided proper maintenance is performed.

8.   Notation is made that WP shell, stored horizontally in tropical
climates become inaccurate by phosphorus collecting on the bottom side.

   Comment: This defect can be eliminated by storing WP shell in a
              vertical position, point up.

9.   "Impregnated clothing deteriorates very rapidly in the tropics."

Comment: This is true in case of individual garments. However, the life in the tropics of this type clothing is extended if the bales of clothing remain unbroken thus retarding the penetration into the clothing of the factors which produce rapid deterioration.

10. Two other statements are general in nature, viz: (1) In the jungle the radio is not reliable and its range is greatly restricted. (2) The sound power phone is extremely valuable.

Comment: The application of these facts to the fire control equipment of chemical mortar battalions is clear.

SIGNAL COMMUNICATIONS DURING THE HOLLANDIA OPERATION

1. This report covers the activities of a signal battalion and attached troops during the Hollandia Operation.

2. The general plan of operation called for simultaneous landings on the beaches of Tanamerah and Humboldt Bay, to be followed by a rapid thrust inland in a pincers movement to capture the airdromes north and west of Lake Sentani.

3. Narrative: a. Signal Operations.

(1) D-day.

(a) H-hour, D-day was 0700, 22 April 1944. The D-day personnel and equipment were divided among four LST's which beached on Red Beach #2, Tanamerah Bay at 0815. Red Beach #2 was much narrower than had been anticipated. The roads indicated on the map were only tracks. The terrain was not suited for rapid road construction. As a result, traffic along the beach became congested and unloading proceeded very slowly. Only one battalion vehicle reached the command post. The others were scattered along the beach unable to move. Except for chauffeurs, a few radio operators and cryptographic clerks, all signal personnel proceeded on foot down the beach to the site of the proposed task force command post. The message center was established immediately, a small area cleared and foxholes dug. Radio contact with division command post afloat was established at 1130 using a radio set SCR-299 set up on the top deck of an LST. At 1430, command post was set up ashore near that of the task force. Wire circuits were installed and in operation by 1530. Due to the proximity of the two command posts ashore the radio net was closed at 1800.

(b) During the day a net of five radio sets SCR-300 kept a fifteen minute schedule. Stations in the net were the task force signal officer on the headquarters ship, an assistant task force signal officer ashore, a liaison officer of a signal battalion ashore, an assistant task force G-3 ashore and task force G-3 on division headquarters ship. Considerable difficulty was experienced in delivering messages as the majority of the staff had not yet located at the command post ashore.

(c) About 1730 at AT-20 radio transmitter mounted in a 2½ ton truck was landed. Using this set, an attempt was made to establish radio contact with task forces at the Admiralty Islands and Aitape without success probably due to the use of an unsuitable frequency. About the same time another AT-20 transmitter, mounted in a van, entered the army net. Intermittent contact was maintained throughout the night.

(2) D ≠ 1:

(a) Radio contact with both divisions and the task force headquarters ship was established early. Radio contact, using an AT-20 radio transmitter, was maintained with army. At 1000 radio contact was established readily with the task forces at the Admiralty Islands and Aitape using a radio set SCR-299 on a frequency different from that previously assigned.

(b) Due to the congestion of the beaches of Tanamerah Bay, the task force commander decided to move the task force command post to the Humboldt Bay area. All stations closed at 1530 for reloading on LST's. Loading was twice interrupted by air alerts but all personnel and equipment were aboard by 2300. Water movement to White Beach #3 started at 2330. The D-day detachment of the construction platoon was directed to remain at Red Beach #2 to extend spiral-four cable. It was used by one division to extend its field wire lines.

(3) D ≠ 2:

All personnel remained aboard the LST's until the morning of D ≠ 3. While the task force command post was still afloat, the navy monitored the task force radio channels and copied messages addressed to the task force. Navy cryptographic personnel was not sufficient to handle the task force traffic as well as their own.

(4) D ≠ 3:

(a) After landing, the unloading proceeded fairly rapidly, using all battalion personnel except radio operators and cryptographic clerks. By 1000 the task force command net and one radio circuit to army were in operation.

(b) One cryptographic clerk from the battalion was sent to assist the navy in handling intercepted task force radio traffic. Even with this additional help cryptographic

personnel could not keep abrest of their work and sent fifty
undeciphered messages to the task force. In order to
decipher this traffic according to proper precedence, it
was necessary to continually change the pin and lug settings
of converter M-209 and the strip arrangement of Cipher
Device M-138. This, in addition to normal traffic and
poor working conditions made for relatively slow work.
Several days passed before the cryptographic section was
completely caught up.

(c) At 1500 two radio teams, the message center section and
small detachments of the other sections left White Beach #3
for Brinkmans Plantation via Pim. This was the new location of the task force command post. Installation was
started immediately upon arrival. Radio nets were established, switchboard and essential locals installed and a wire
circuit to a second division command post near Joka initially established through the division's artillery command
post at Brinkmans Plantation. During the night battalion
personnel manned a part of the command post defense line.
Radio and message center blacked out but continued to
operate.

(d) The intelligence and maintenance section of the wire
operation company, in the absence of the two organic construction companies, started installation of trunks to
attached corps units, a radar station on Leimok Hill and
to Pim. A traffic control line was installed along the
Pim-Joka Road. The reinforced platoon installed field
wire trunks to the division command post, one mile east
of Joka. Trouble crews were kept busy twenty-four hours
a day repairing circuits destroyed by tractors, bulldozers,
our own troops and natives clearing bivouac areas.

(5) D $\neq$ 3 and D $\neq$ 4:

(a) A telephone central office set TC-12 was installed. The
next day a second switchboard BD-91 was added. The switchboard installation was dug in and well sandbagged.

(b) Initial plans for teletype operation called for the installation of one teletypewriter set EE-97 at the message
center connected by a simplex circuit to the division.
Due to leakage and unbalance the simplex circuit had to be
abandoned. A phantom circuit was substituted but construction work on the Pim-Joka Road continually tore out the
field wire lines. Teletype operation had to be abandoned
until a third field wire circuit to the division had been
installed over an alternate route. Even then satisfactory
operation was not obtained.

(6) D $\neq$ 5 to D $\neq$ 9:

Radio facilities in operation were: two circuits (point-to-point) to army using two AT-20 radio transmitters, one of which was later replaced by a radio set SCR-339-G; one circuit linking the task force with those at the Admiralty Islands and Aitape, using first radio set SCR-299 and later a TW-12 radio transmitter; two command nets, one using a radio set SCR-299 to one division only and the other using a radio set SCR-177 to all units; an aircraft warning net using radio set SCR-193; and an intercept station on the navy "Dog" circuit. Transmitters had been remoted to improve readability. Some confusion existed among units which had entered the command net because of difficulty in distributing items of SOI covering pin and lug settings for converter M-209 common to all units.

(7) D ≠ 10:

    (a) The two divisions established new command posts on D ≠ 10 in preparation for another operation. To establish wire communication to one division about half the platoon from a signal construction battalion, aviation, started installation of a spiral-four cable from the command post at Brinkmans Plantation around the south side of Jauntefa Bay to Hollekang, a distance of approximately ten miles. There were no roads through the area and most of the route was through swamp and heavily timbered rain forest. Dumps of spiral-four cable had to be established along the beaches and the cable handcarried to the route about one-half mile inland. Considerable trouble developed on this line due to defective cable and cutting by our own troops and natives. To supplement this circuit, a spiral-four cable was laid under water from Pim to White Beach #3. This proved to be a more reliable circuit. Another detachment of a signal construction battalion put in two spiral-four circuits from Brinkmans Plantation to the site of a proposed task force command post at Joka on Lake Sentani.

    (b) A detachment of the battalion consisting of 2 officers and 50 enlisted men moved to Joka to set up the new command post. Signal installation and construction of temporary buildings to house communication facilities was started.

    (c) In the command post area ten-pair cables were fanned out to various office sites so that only short runs of field wire would be needed. Two telephone central office sets TC-2 were installed. Ten-pair and five-pair cables were run to a test station (Lake Test) at the road junction of the Joka and Airdrome Roads.

(8) D ≠ 12:

    (a) Adequate messenger service had been difficult to maintain.

Units were distributed over a number of beaches and along congested tracks. Boat transportation only could reach the beaches. Units moving along the tracks were frequently delayed and bivouacked along the road in a new location each night. Messengers carried all personal equipment and rations as in many instances they were out for two or three days. Messengers brought back valuable information as to the location of units. Liaison airplanes were used to carry messages to isolated areas. To facilitate message delivery, message sub-centers were set up. All messages to units on the beaches were delivered to a message sub-center at Pim. Messengers located there hitch-hiked by boat from beach to beach. A message sub-center was established also in the airdrome area. Later, in addition to local message delivery, personnel of this message sub-center had the duty of receiving, collecting and guarding signal supplies arriving by air transport. Due to the above-mentioned difficulties, a DUKW was made available to the message center on D $\neq$ 12. Located at Pim, this vehicle made it possible to establish schedule messenger service to the beaches and greatly improved message delivery.

(b) Up to D $\neq$ 12, no scheduled safehand service could be established. All available means of transportation were used. Local collection and delivery of safehand was made by authorized enlisted personnel, no courier officers being available. Starting on D $\neq$ 12 a daily schedule was established by the task force. A courier officer flew by air transport from the task force to the army headquarters and returned the following day. Normally this service is operated by USASOS. Safehand was an additional responsibility now placed on the message center.

(9) D $\neq$ 13:

A spiral-four cable with a test point installed on the island was laid across Lake Sentani from Joka to a point near Cyclops Drome. An LVT was used to make the submarine installation. A waterproof splice for the spiral-four cable was developed. On D $\neq$ 16 a second cable to a bombardment wing near Cyclops Drome and on D $\neq$ 23 a third cable providing a through circuit for air warning between the radar station on Leimok Hill and an AAA group near Cyclops Drome were installed over the same route. The only interruption of service was caused by a seaplane anchor breaking one cable.

(10) D $\neq$ 16:

(a) Switchboards BD-72 and locals were installed at Pim and at Pie Beach. A telephone central office set TC-12 was substituted at Pie Beach the following day.. At this stage, field wire installed initially was being replaced gradually by spiral-four cable or new field wire.

(b) Four converters M-134-D were delivered by courier officer. Two machines were immediately set up at the command post at Brinkmans Plantation and the other two at the site to be occupied by the new command post at Joka. Until then only manual cryptographic systems were used. Daily group count of enciphered and deciphered traffic for the first week averaged slightly less than 10,000 groups, then slowly increased to about 17,000 by D $\neq$ 40. Approximately two-thirds of the traffic was handled by converter M-209 and one-third by strip cipher. The prohibition on the use of converter M134-D during the "hazardous duty" phase greatly slowed cryptographic operations. Efforts were made to have messages written so as to permit confidential classification and thereby allow encipherment by converter M-209. On the other hand the use of clear text radio messages was discouraged. In the task force headquarters all clear text radio messages had to be countersigned by the chief or deputy chief of staff. Message authentication was not used to subordinate units but was used to higher headquarters. Telephone authentication was seldom used.

(11) D $\neq$ 17:

A telegraph central office set TC-3 and teletypewriter set CE-97 were installed at Joka and two spiral-four cables phantomed to give two teletype circuits to Brinkmans Plantation which was to remain as the task force rear echelon command post and later to be occupied by Base "G", USASOS.

(12) D $\neq$ 20:

The command post at Joka opened. Cut over was very successful no interruption of communications resulting. There were few men available to clear the battalion area, erect mess halls, supply buildings, etc. This work proceeded slowly and was further hampered by battalion having to furnish daily four to ten $\frac{3}{4}$-ton trucks for hauling signal supplies and for corps details.

(13) D $\neq$ 21 to D $\neq$ 23:

Up to this date the message center section was handicapped greatly by the lack of sufficient personnel and sheltered operating space. Except during inclement weather and at night, several men had to work outside. During air alerts the message center continued to operate but blackout and overcrowding reduced its efficiency. Up to D $\neq$ 16 the message center had forty men men available exclusive of messengers. Only twenty men were from the battalion message center section; the balance was made up of seven teletype operators from the battalion, ten men from a radio team and three men borrowed from a signal service company. On D $\neq$ 16 nine men from another radio team arrived

but they left on D / 21. On that date eleven message
center and cryptographic clerks from a signal operation
battalion were attached. On D / 23 nine additional
cryptographic clerks were borrowed from the signal service
company and nine men from an infantry company were attached.
The latter were used as message center guards and local
messengers. This additional personnel was sufficient to
operate the task force and three message sub-centers.
Some confusion existed as the attached personnel was from
five units, one of which joined just prior to, and the
other four during the operation. No joint training prior
to the operation was possible as the units were dispersed
over a large area. Because of the minor differences of
procedure smooth functioning was not obtained. About this
date the advance section of army arrived. Pending establishment of the army command post near Hollekang, a
separate message center group was set up to handle
exclusively the army traffic. Traffic of base section "G"
had to be handled also until base facilities were installed
about D / 45.

(14) **D / 25 to D / 33:**

(a) On D / 25 battalion personnel began handling the army
traffic for another operation. The following additional
radio circuits were established: one to the army and
advance GHQ using a radio set SCR-299; one to the site
of the other operation and army using an AT-20 radio
transmitter; and two to the other operation using one
radio set SCR-299 and one TW-12 radio transmitter.

(b) Four telephone terminal sets TC-21 and eight telegraph
terminal sets TC-22 were received. All had to be completely
overhauled and it was not until D / 33 that two carrier
circuits were in operation to the command post of the
advance section of the army near Hollekang. Teletype
operation was satisfactory but failure of ringing equipment EE-101-A prevented the use of the channels for voice
transmission. Defective varistors in ringing equipment
EE-101-A had to be replaced by a vacuum tube rectifier
assembly.

(c) During the period D / 25 to D / 30 five field wire circuits
were installed across Lake Sentani to various units. The
reinforced platoon, company B of a signal construction
battalion aviation put in a two mile pole line from
Brinkmans Plantation to Leimok Hill using 35-foot poles
logged locally. This line was for later use by Base "G".
Assisted by twenty natives to clear a right of way this
unit also installed a spiral-four cable around the north
side of Lake Sentani from Lake Test to a bombardment wing.
Company B of another signal construction battalion aviation
cleared a right of way and set poles for a permanent pole
line from Lake Test to Joka, installed eight miles of spiral-

four cable from Brinkmans Plantation to the town where the command post of an infantry regiment and a navy PT base were located and installed spiral-four cable over a water and land route from Pim to Pie Beach. Teletype to the naval liaison party was in operation by D $\neq$ 33.

b. Signal Supply:

(1) Signal supply was the responsibility of the task force. The battalion S-4 was designated as the task force signal supply officer. A signal dump was established on D $\neq$ 9 at Pie Beach and was operated by the provisional storage and issue section and a detachment of one officer and 33 men from an infantry regiment. Construction of shelter and location of signal supplies dumped at random along the beaches was given first consideration. Stock levels were low so only emergency issues were made. Transfer of the stock from Pie Beach to the permanent base signal depot at Brinkmans Plantation was difficult. Water transportation was furnished by LCM and LCT to Pim but transfer was slow until a road from Pie Beach to Pim was opened.

(2) As soon as the airdromes were serviceable, large quantities of all kinds of supplies were sent in by air transport. The road to the airdromes was not opened until D $\neq$ 23. Supplies unloaded from the air transports were dumped in the drome area.

c. Battalion Supply:

The battalion supply section had little activity. This permitted the release of a few men to the signal intelligence officer, USAFFE. Under his direction, the men collected, serviced, packed and shipped to Australia for reshipment to the United States a large quantity of captured Japanese signal equipment.

d. Battalion Medical Detachment:

(1) The battalion aid station was set up initially at Brinkmans' Plantation. It also served other units attached to the task force, elements of two divisions in the vicinity and foreign civilian and military personnel released from capture. A large number of Hindu soldiers who had been captured were treated for malaria, dysentery and tropical ulcers. A large number of wounded Japanese prisoners were also received for treatment pending questioning by the task force G-2.

(2) During the period covered by this report about 125 cases were handled daily by the battalion medical detachment. Evacuation from forward and to rear areas was also handled by the detachment.

e. Miscellaneous:

(1) Signal communication was not interrupted to any great extent by enemy activity. There were indications that some line

troubles were caused by the enemy. No enemy jamming of radio was experienced.

(2) Personnel leaving the command post were always armed. Although messengers and linemen were often near Japanese patrols they were never attacked.

(3) The tactical situation was ideal for the use of pigeons. Australian birds and equipment had been furnished the battalion; birds arrived on D $\neq$ 2. They were settled at Brinkmans Plantation but not used. Initial use was on D $\neq$ 21 after they had been moved to Joka and settled. Starting on D $\neq$ 33 they were furnished daily to patrols. The pigeons brought back many important operational messages. Troops have gained confidence in and like to use the homing pigeon.

(4) Japanese gasoline was used to supplement our own limited supply. This gasoline proved detrimental to power units as it caused excessive carbon deposits.

4. Observations: The following observations are based on the difficulties encountered and experience gained during the operation.

a. Wire W-110 laid in salt water lasted only from three to four days but spiral-four cable stood up well with only minor trouble. Wire W-110 gave satisfactory service when laid in fresh water. Spiral-four cable was easier to maintain than wire W-110 but unless it was placed on poles, service interruptions were inevitable.

b. Cable routes in shallow water and at anchorages must be plainly marked.

c. D-7 bulldozers, power drills, saws and jack hammers should be authorized all signal construction units in this type of theater if reliable wire communications are to be established early.

d. Where great use is made of radio the resulting heavy cryptographic load necessitates an increase in the number of message center and cryptographic clerks. The message center should have at least thirty-five cryptographic and fifteen message clerks.

e. Five message center officers, at least, are required. One officer must be on duty at all times at the forward echelon. The section leader should be free to handle the section administration and exercise general supervision over its operation.

f. Joint training of all signal personnel engaged in an operation is necessary if smooth functioning is to be obtained.

g. Previous training of messengers in map reading and during maneuvers and command post exercises paid dividends.

h. A map plot of unit locations is very valuable to all staff sections. Messengers can furnish information needed to keep the map up-to-date.

i. Brevity codes are valuable in circumventing the use of plain language of radio.

j. At least one **cipher** key common to all units of a task force must be distributed prior to an operation.

k. Selection and assignment of radio channels must consider predicted radio propagation conditions if reliable radio communication at all ranges is to be maintained.

l. Better protection of terminals and top layer of cable of spiral-four cable is required to withstand the rough handling incident to an amphibious operation.

m. Training of service troops in the proper method of defense against infiltration by the enemy must be emphasized. New troops usually become "trigger-happy" unless rigid control is exercised.

AMPHIBIOUS SUPPLY

Supplies were moved ashore as needed by the combat troops with the result that beaches were kept clear throughout the operation. A supply point was established on one island after it was secured in order to unload one transport division which was to be released as quickly as possible. Practically all supplies landed behind the combat troops were transported in DUKW's. For this purpose the service companies of two infantry regiments were formed and trained as DUKW companies. Supplies were usually delivered direct to battalion dumps. DUKW's were routed through regimental points, where, on occasion, rearrangement of loads was made to fit the supply needs of the battalions. Movements of supplies ashore was controlled during the initial phase by an assistant G-4 aboard the control vessel who had radio communication with shore and the transports. The G-4 was located on the ship with the commodore of the transports. The end of the operation found approximately one-third of the supplies still aboard the transports. At no time were the troops lacking in any type of needed supplies.

ORDNANCE SUBJECTS

I. ORDNANCE AT A BEACHHEAD

1. In this operation ordnance maintenance service in the initial phases was provided by detachments from one ordnance medium maintenance company (Q) which landed about 0900 D-day. On D ∕ 3 all ordnance units except this company were released from engineer shore regiments and placed under corps control; it was left for the purpose of maintaining DUKW's and other vehicles around beachheads. As time went on the detachments were built up, by the arrival of the balance of each company, to full strength medium maintenance companies. All the detachments with the exception of one were without proper tools and equipment for the first three or four days. For this reason they were powerless to do little more than second echelon work with only hand tools and practically no spare parts.

2. The medium maintenance company was primarily set up to maintain DUKWs during the initial phases. Their technical vehicles and tools were not landed until the afternoon of D / 3 at which time two days' back log of work was on hand. While without tools their time was spent mainly in helping with small repair jobs and in doing a little de-water-proofing. This company found that welding was needed and used continuously in DUKW maintenance. Although the company had hot patch tube repair equipment, it was used very little, owing to higher priority of heavier work. Most of their patches were issued to second echelon units. Salvaged DUKW's became a valuable source of spare parts. It was found that in a detachment of this sort, all the men initially landed should be mechanics. Wreckers are essential in maintaining DUKWs and should be one of the first items of ordnance equipment landed.

3. One ordnance company detachment had more tools and equipment on hand for use during the first few days than did any of the others. The technical vehicles for this company, the bulk of the company and about 200 tons of supplies landed on D / 3. On D / 8 this one company was still the main part of the corps ordnance battalion. Practically all the parts and major items issue and the bulk of the maintenance work for the battalion was done by this company. Detachments from other companies which were still without tools and equipment were attached to this company to increase its output. Most of the major items and parts available for issue to troops during the first five or six days were those brought by this company. In addition, many major items and assemblies were repaired and reissued during this period. This company found that their greatest shortages were in combat vehicle parts, instrument parts and artillery parts.

4. One detachment of a medium maintenance company (Q) was without proper tools and equipment and set itself up in an engineer motor pool to use engineer tools. A lot of good repair work was done by this detachment. Their only source of spare parts during the first five or six days was cannibalized vehicles. No ordnance tools were available to them until D / 4 when a portion of their vehicles arrived. There was much 3d echelon automotive work to be done from D / 1 onwards.

5. The detachment whose primary mission was AA maintenance had very little call for work during the first five or six days. No tools or equipment for doing this work were available. A 3/4-ton truck belonging to this detachment was landed D-day but was not located until D / 3. This truck contained tools and some small arms parts. On D / 3 the small arms repair truck arrived.

6. These several detachments landed with very little equipment and parts and operating independently of one another could not render proper and efficient ordnance service. Wreckers should be among the first vehicles landed. As many major items as possible, particularly small arms and artillery, should be brought in with the unit. There is no need for ordnance units being brought in before sometime in the late morning of D / 1. A small detachment, with transportation, should be landed in the afternoon of D-day for the purpose of selecting an area in which to set up the "reinforced" company and to post signs on all beaches and roads indicating the route to the ordnance area. This is necessary because units are as

often as not landed on a beach different from the one for which they were originally scheduled. If it is necessary that ordnance maintenance be provided in more than one location, detachments from the "reinforced" company should be set up wherever necessary, the heavier work being carried to the company area where facilities can be used to best advantage. A unified command for ordnance service during the initial phases provides a flexibility and control which is not possible with several detachments operating independently of one another. As time goes on, the balance of each company which furnished detachments for small arms, artillery, and tank maintenance should be brought in and these companies, when built up to sufficient strength, separated from the original "reinforced" (Q) company. Ordnance personnel should in all cases be moved on the same ship as their equipment so that personnel and equipment will be together at all times after landing and will thus be able to start functioning sooner.

7. Several ordnance companies possessed illuminated signs which were set up at main road intersections indicating the company location. Such a sign should be as easily distinguished in daylight as in darkness. 3/4-ton vehicles used by ordnance contact parties which are well marked with ordnance insignia and colors create the impression that ordnance is "on the job" in the neighborhood and helps "sell" the idea that ordnance units are pushing their services out to combat troops.

8. A detachment of an ordnance depot company landed at 1900 on D Day. This outfit had no supplies to handle until the night D ∤ 2 when the 200 tons of major items and parts for another ordnance company began to arrive. On the afternoon of D ∤ 3, depot supplies started arriving. Supplies continued to arrive 24 hours a day until the night of D ∤ 10 when delivery of ordnance supplies to the company after dark was stopped. This small detachment was greatly handicapped by a complete lack of transportation. The number of men (13) was so small that proper sorting of supplies during the night, when no lights of any kind were allowed, was impossible. The next morning, many signal and engineer supplies would be found haphazardly mixed with ordnance boxes. In order to prevent excessive fatigue and consequent inefficiency initial depot detachment should consist of 35 or 40 men. A depot detachment should be landed with a 1/4-ton truck and several 2½-ton trucks with winch, each equipped with an "A" frame wich mounts on front of frame and can be used with winch in lifting, sorting and stacking ordnance items in the depot dump. The ¼-ton truck is badly needed for searching beaches and other dumps for supplies known to have been shipped but which do not show up at the dump. The company stated that during the first two weeks many supplies which they knew had been shipped in the first boats had not shown up at their dump. Since no transportation was available, they could not search elsewhere for these supplies nor could they notify other services to pick up supplies erroneously brought to ordnance dump and which were in their way. This detachment even had trouble getting rations and water due to lack of transportation.

9. There were many demands for ¼-ton truck tires and tubes, and motorcycle tires and tubes, which could not be filled. Many 7.50 x 20 tires without tubes were on hand. Supplying tires without tubes during the first few weeks of an amphibious operation is a mistake. After landings, tires are needed to replace damaged items, not worn ones. When tires are damaged sufficiently to require replacement, tubes are usually ruined also. Initially, tires and tubes should be supplied in equal quantities and should be shipped together.

10. There were unsatisfied demands for small automotive parts such as distributors, distributor parts, distributor heads, high tension wiring, spark plugs, spring for generator and starter brushes, brake parts, etc. A large majority of the small parts demanded were those which are most likely to be damaged by application or removal of waterproofing materials or by action of sea water. All ignition parts, exposed electrical parts (such as those for generators and starters) and other parts which are likely to be damaged by waterproofing or wading should be supplied in large quantities in the early part of an amphibious operation.

11. A and B group items were received early and there was a fairly large demand for these items.

12. This depot company stated that it was not furnished a weapons list of the units which they were to support so that it could intelligently stock correct quantities of items and parts.

13. During the first few days the depot company issued available spare parts for any item to anyone who came to the depot requesting parts, regardless of rank or organization. This practice was wrong. Parts should be issued only through maintenance companies so as to get the most from exchange of serviceable and unserviceable items and insure that a minimum of repairable parts are thrown away or not gotten into the hands of an ordnance unit.

II. AMPHIBIOUS ORDNANCE EXPERIENCE

1. The following summary of the activities and experiences of one light maintenance company in the Pacific area from 23 July to 9 August 1943 is typical of other ordnance organizations in this area.

a. The company was split into forward and rear echelons: The forward being composed of the small arms, ammunition and artillery sections and the rear echelon being comprised of the automotive and depot sections.

    (1) Supply and service was maintained between the various islands by boat and from beaches to island points by $\frac{1}{4}$-ton vehicles.
    (2) The artillery sections, operating from one of the beaches, serviced the division artillery located on an island offshore.
    (3) The division ammunition distributing point was located with the forward echelon. Two units of fire for all type infantry weapons were maintained at this point. Artillery ammunition supply was under the direction of the corps artillery officer

b. A small arms shop was set up at the forward echelon for the receipt, repair, salvage of materiel and issuance of major items, accessories and cleaning and preserving materials. A cleaning bench with table was set up allowing the casual soldier to clean and service his weapon. Two instrument men (non T/O) were kept constantly busy in cleaning and making much needed repairs. Salvage crews were dispatched daily to service companies of the regiments, returning to this area to repair weapons collected during the day's work. Constant contact was maintained with the combat units to assure repair and replacement of weapons.

ENGINEER SUBJECTS

I. ARMY REPORT

1. It is not intended that the report be complete in all respects, or present a detailed narrative of the campaign from an engineer standpoint. It is rather an attempt to assemble the information and experience gained, so that similar headquarters may profit thereby.

2. Planning.

   a. An adequate staff must be available immediately to permit the detailed study of all possible needs. For an operation of this size organized with the base area group as an integral part of the command, an engineer staff for a reinforced corps is adequate if supplemented by a few key members of the base area group, and, for short periods of the planning stage, for detailed technical advice by liaison officers from special engineer units. Requirements for troops and supplies needed in a planned operation must be based upon a reasonable amount of experience, and a knowledge of the responsibilities of the various organizations as well as the capabilities of the various troop units, their personnel, and equipment and the supplies required to permit efficient operation in the field.

   b. Future moves must be included in any directive upon which planning is to be based. Failing that, at least an estimate must be established to provide a basis for planning and to insure coordination of all concerned. Initial planning must provide for subsequent moves to carry the operation to its logical conclusion, which might either be another operation to exploit success, or the cessation of active operations and the establishment of a supply base or bases.

   c. Relation of time. Critical items of Engineer Class IV Supply require at least ninety days between requisition and delivery. The mission must be defined in ample time to complete plans whose execution demand these items.

3. Training - The Army engineer section was only involved in the training to a limited extent. This consisted primarily in general supervision of the training of shore regiments of the amphibian brigade. During the later stages of the training period, attempt was made to guide the training of miscellaneous ASF engineer units scheduled to join the task force at some later date. Training for the landings was decentralized to the sub task forces and no attempt was made to supervise closely the training of combat engineer units directly under corps or division headquarters. Training was continuously inspected, however, and constructive criticism furnished the army chief of staff. Assistance was provided by the army engineer section in the form of experimentation and dissemination of all available information on assault tactics against a hostile shore.

   a. Experimentation must be completed prior to the commencement of the training period, of failing that, be conducted by troops other than those involved in the operation. Continual changes in the standard operating procedures of the various types of engineer units can lead only to confusion and a failure to complete proper training.

b. The training program preparing troops for active operations must not be interrupted or interfered with by numerous demonstrations that disrupt training schedules involving both services and take valuable time from training periods.

c. Components of beach groups must be assembled early to permit the coordination and training necessary for efficient operation. Sufficient time therefore should be provided to establish standard operating procedures and develop necessary teamwork. This applies particularly to military police who are to control traffic across mined beaches.

d. Realism in training is essential regardless of the risk to personnel and equipment. Unless some attempt is made to reproduce enemy action and erect obstacles likely to be encountered in combat, training will fail to prepare each soldier to meet any eventuality.

4. Loading of supplies - The rapid accumulation of supplies from numerous widespread sources and the lack of detailed information on ship arrivals and departures prevented a comprehensive plan for the loading of engineer supplies. Pipeline equipment and materials were considered to be the critical items requiring special attention and personnel of the section were assigned the specific mission of supervising their loading. Principal items of a combat nature were made available to sub task force and loaded according to the decisions of sub task force commanders.

a. Control of the loading of personnel, supplies and equipment should not be too greatly decentralized. The possibility of assumption of control at an early date by the higher headquarters demands adequate control to insure proper arrival of troops and supplies based on the overall picture. The advisability of the task force retaining a small part of the shipping space provided each sub task force until all last minute requirements are known should be considered to provide for unexpected late demands on the task force as a whole.

b. Loading of items of a complicated or highly technical nature must be supervised by personnel capable of identifying parts and who realize the necessity for orderly placement on shipboard. A Bailey bridge lacking an essential part might better remain on the dock in a base area than take up valuable space on a transport.

c. Prime movers and trailers must be loaded on the same craft with the equipment they move. Valuable time is lost in the preparation of beach roads and dumps if the tractors of shore regiments are used as prime movers in the unloading of LCT's and LST's.

5. Landing - Methods of landings and schedules of operations during the first several days of the operation were planned and controlled by the individual sub task force commanders working in cooperation with corresponding naval sub task forces.

a. Engineer personnel with mine detectors or personnel trained in prodding (a ramrod is good in the sand) must precede vehicles coming ashore. Mines were encountered on practically all beaches and valuable equipment was lost because of a failure on the part of beach groups to properly provide for their removal prior to the arrival of motor equipment.

b. Adequate traffic control personnel and a large quantity of signs should be landed early. Confusion can be eliminated and traffic channeled to follow mine cleared lanes only by proper sign posting and control of traffic.

c. Centralized control of unloading and the consolidation of supply dumps should be effected at the earliest possible moment consistent with tactical needs even preceding the assumption of command by the task force.

d. Beach markers must be simple. Flank markers to define the limits of the beach, landing points markers and road exist markers for vehicle and DUKW drivers are all that are required.

6. Operations - Thus far all engineer units have been used generally in the role for which organized. Exception to this was the use of elements of two engineer regiments in an infantry role during the first few days.

a. All personnel should be trained to make maximum use of halazone tablets and hypochloride capsules when providing themselves with water. Engineers are thereby relieved from establishing water points for isolated areas.

b. Photo interpretation by a trained officer is of great value in the planning of combat engineer work in the forward echelons. Interpretation of air-photographs by an expert from an engineer point of view has been of value in giving advance information of demolitions, mine fields and defensive installations.

c. It should be made clear to civilian agencies with the task force that they must work through the task force engineer as long as operations require.

d. All personnel should have a greater appreciation of the value of maps. Unreasonable requests for maps during the operation probably resulted because initial issues were generous, giving the impression that maps were available to be expended as desired.

7. Organization.

a. An organization trained in the nomenclature, care, transportation and erection of the Bailey bridge as a heavy ponton company is trained to handle the ponton bridge is highly desirable.

b. One of the most vital functions of the engineers during the operation has been the supply of maps. The volume, because of the unexpectedly large number of troops concentrated in a small area has been tremendous. In many instances additional personnel was required to assist the small map depot detachments in the sorting, packaging and issue of maps. In addition, with a rapidly moving force the map supply must be mobile so that maps are steadily available when and where called for.

8. <u>Supply and equipment</u> - Thus far little difficulty has been encountered in meeting our needs for essential supplies. The situation has been considerably aided by the availability of a large amount of captured enemy materials. D-7 angledozers have proved inadequate for the requirements of the terrain encountered. Shortages in a few important items are gradually being relieved by pooling and transfers between units, including aviation engineers who have been most helpful and cooperative.

9. a. <u>All requisitions of engineer equipment must accompany units on their initial landing or an early convoy thereafter.</u> Engineers require specialized equipment in order to accomplish normal missions of road repair and the construction of bypasses and bridges. Lack of this equipment may make it impossible to perform the role for which organized.

b. Bailey bridges should be available early in the operation. Upon the ability of the engineers to rapidly bypass or repair demolished bridges largely determines the rapidity of progress of the artillery, general equipment and of the operation as a whole. Adequate facilities to accomplish this mission should be available from the beginning.

c. Additional end pieces for Bailey bridges should be provided in this type of terrain. This need is obvious when it is realized that the greater number of bridges erected have been in lengths of less than the bridge unit of 120'.

II. AIR PHOTOGRAPHS

1. The army headquarters engineer photographic section had as its prime interest the serving of using troops. In one noteworthy incident, photographs were delivered to an armored division within $3\frac{1}{2}$ hours of the time the pilot was briefed.

2. A Photographic Interpreters School was established at the theater photo reconnaissance wing.

3. This headquarters concurs in the recommendation that the aircraft allotted for army photographic missions be equipped with longer focal length cameras. The 36" camera, upon which experiments were conducted during the campaign appears to be the answer to this problem. Enemy positions are more easily found on photographs taken with a 36" camera.

4. The providing of controlled mosaics is an engineer function and these should be prepared in advance while the operation is in its planning stage.

5. During the planning phase all photo intelligence is strategic and all personnel and facilities must be controlled by the headquarters responsible for the operations as a whole. Interpretation, likewise, must be centrally located during this period.

6. It is necessary, from the engineer's point of view, to place an engineer photo interpreter with the division section, corps section and army section at the airfield. Likewise artillery counterbattery officers will be placed with each section.

III. BRIDGES

1. Army comments: "The Bailey bridge should be organic down to and including the corps engineer regiment. We keep eight bridges at all times in the army dump. One corps has on hand, ready to move at all times, three Bailey bridges, each 130 feet long, double double; another corps, two. When they run out they call back to our dump and fill up. Each corps should have at all times a number of bridges available. As soon as we can we replace Bailey bridges with a permanent bridge. We have no substitute for the Bailey bridge, and until we get some, we will have to use it."

2. Corps comments: "Bailey bridges should be by all means stocked down to and including the corps bridge brigade."

"Bailey bridges have been life-savers. We can't get enough of them. The 30-ton ponton bridge of the armored force units has also proved invaluable."

3. Division engineer units in the States should be trained in laying the Bailey bridge. For this purpose, as training aids, there should be one Bailey bridge per combat battalion and one per engineer regiment. Division engineer units do not need to stock Bailey bridges in the combat zone if they are available to the corps engineer. Once in a while the division combat engineer battalion has to set up Bailey bridges.

4. Stress putting in bridges at night. You can not do that job in the day time when under observed fire. Stress movement, including driver training, proper intervals between vehicles and prevention of double banking.

5. We found the plywood treadway bridge, which used to be with the division, very useful. They should be available to divisions. This treadway bridge can be laid on the infantry assault raft. We use the regular 6-ton and 12-ton floats with the plywood treadway.

IV. REPORT OF ACTIVITIES AND CRITIQUES OF EQUIPMENT ENGINEER MAINTENANCE COMPANY

1. Deviation from S.O.P. in employment of equipment.

The mobility of the machine shops, electrical repair shops, small tool repair shops and tool and bench shops has not been utilized to a very great extent due to the tactical situation. It has been found that an overhead shelter constructed in the shop area utilizing timber and poles for framework and tarpaulin or corrugated sheeting for covering, has contributed greatly to the working efficiency of the shop platoons in this climate. The welding shops have done a considerable amount of work outside of the shop area and the emergency repair trucks work around the clock in exercising preventive maintenance.

One of the three welding shops assigned to the contact platoon has been reassigned to the second maintenance platoon and one additional cargo truck has been assigned to the contact platoon. One additional Hobart welder has been obtained and assigned to the first maintenance platoon. It is mounted on a standard cargo trailer. The forges are not mounted in the welding shops.

One standard emergency repair truck is yet to be received. As the others were received the improvised ones mounted on the 3/4-ton weapons carrier were retained in service and are in constant use.

One additional lubrication trailer has been authorized. It will be assigned to the contact platoon.

The blacksmith trailers have been reduced to cargo trailers as they have not been necessary.

One additional heavy lathe and a brake lining machine have been received and are assigned to the first maintenance platoon. The lathe has been mounted on a salvaged marine four wheel Spencer trailer.

A Japanese prime mover (6x6) truck has been fitted up as a light wrecker by the contact platoon. The contact platoon also operates a Japanese truck (equivalent to a weapon carrier) and a Ford dump truck which were salvaged.

A number of other vehicles abandoned by combat troops have been reclaimed from salvage from time to time.

The first maintenance platoon is rather widely dispersed on a number of outlying islands. That platoon has rehabilitated a Japanese armored barge. This has a ramp and will be able to move a 2½-ton, 6x6, truck between the islands readily and will greatly increase the efficiency of the emergency repair and welding shops of that platoon.

At the present time a 15kw generator is being used to power the shops of the two platoons.

2. <u>Duties not normally anticipated for a Maintenance Company.</u>

Due to the ever changing tactical situation the limited maintenance facilities of other branches of the service during periods of construction and organization on the different islands, this unit has done a considerable amount of work in addition to its prime function. A crew was furnished to rehabilitate and provide for the initial operation of a saw mill during and immediately subsequent to the combat period. Construction and servicing of utilities was accomplished for the various service commands prior to establishment of the respective utilities detachments. Motor repair and overhauls have been accomplished for navy boat pools in the forward area when local facilities were inadequate. Prior to receipt of the unit's tools and equipment a considerable amount of assistance was given ordnance units in assembling and repairing vehicles. Considerable repair work is done on signal corps and air corps generator units.

This unit furnished personnel and equipment for servicing and transshipping engineer equipment at the different stations. The unit supply section operated the service command spare parts warehouse prior to its being operated by SOS. At the present time the supply section is operating the spare parts section of the advance engineer depot at this station and the unit services and handles transshipment of engineer equipment through this station. The unit also services service command tractors and cranes operating the beach installations at this station.

3. Present condition of unit equipment.

At the present time the unit has essentially all of its T/E equipment except one emergency repair truck. Except for minor repair work dead lining of unit equipment is practically nonexistent. Repair of the unit's ordnance vehicles is accomplished in the unit's shops. Nearly all vehicles have been repainted at least once. The quality of mechanics, electric motor repairmen and machinists within this unit has resulted in the continuous operation and good condition of the generators welders and other equipment of the shops. The damp climate of the tropics with its constant heat and humidity has resulted in unavoidable tarnishing of many polished surfaces of the equipment and tools. This does not apply to the lathe beds and other vital surfaces, however, and the operating efficiency of the equipment has in no way been reduced by this. As the motors in this theater are subject to no abrasive action other than operation on dusty roads, the vehicle motors are in good condition. The mileage of the $2\frac{1}{2}$-ton shop trucks does not exceed one thousand miles and some have accumulated less than five hundred miles. The welding shops and emergency repair shops, of course, have accumulated a somewhat larger mileage. It appears not entirely illogical to assume that with reasonable care, the equipment of this unit could continue to operate for an additional five years without material reduction in efficiency. Such a policy would, of course, necessitate periodic overhaul of the arc welders and generators, and eventually replacement of the generators. This, however, is a relatively simple matter in a theater of operations. As the $2\frac{1}{2}$-ton cargo trucks become worn, the shop truck motors could be changed to the chassis which had accumulated the greater mileage. Under reasonable circumstances new motors are available from the ordnance depots.

One item of equipment which does deteriorate at a noticeable rate, is the canvas tarpaulin on the shop type body. The rate of deterioration exceeds that of the ordnance truck tarpaulin, due to the fact that water does not flow off readily. This defect has been partially remedied by placing additional slats between the bows.

This unit has obtained several portable steel buildings from the services of supply headquarters. These have been dismounted, bundled together and lashed onto the wreckers when platoons move independently thus enabling the work platoon to move "entirely on wheels". Due to the large amount of echelon sets and other accumulated equipment the headquarters platoon can no longer be considered totally mobile. The steel buildings make it possible to rapidly set up a dry supply building, mess hall and shop shelters upon movement to a new location a very important item in this theater.

4. Discussion.

The unit was operating overseas seven months after activation and has been working steadily ever since. More than half of the unit has been operating in a tropical area for nearly one year. Nearly seventy members of the unit have had malaria or dengue fever one or more times. Of this number several have had their usefulness to the unit noticeably reduced.

The equipment of the unit is in good operating condition and under favorable conditions may be considered adequate for the duration of the conflict and any period of occupation to follow.

The same, however, cannot be said of the personnel of the unit. While there is little evidence of the traditional tropical lassitude or slowing down, concessions have to be made frequently for individuals who are in need of additional rest.

While overseas, training has been continuous by means of an informal apprentice system. There is no lack of qualified specialists within this unit. Although the entire unit is employed on repair work at the present time the second maintenance platoon is prepared to move ahead if the tactical situation requires it.

5. Conclusion.

The spare parts problem which definitely has been a problem within this theater at last appears to have a very optimistic future. This change has resulted from the establishment of a spare parts company within the theater.

Although this unit has repeatedly recommended that third echelon sets be formed with an increased proportion of vital items these sets appear to be quite firmly established on the basis of complete overhaul of one machine of each type. Increased depot stocks of vital parts and increased use of air transportation for forward movement of spare parts from these depots may eventually provide a satisfactory solution.

Fundamentally, the allotment of shop equipment and the proportioning of enlisted specialists has proven to be highly satisfactory and generally adequate. Considering the deviation in this theater from the anticipated types of land warfares the original set-up has permitted a gratifying amount of flexibility. The one outstanding deficiency noted has been the lack of a heavy lathe for each of the three work platoons.

It would appear that in these theaters of war the greater proportion of maintenance work may be accomplished at the sites of airfields and road projects. It has been the experience of this unit that the first and second echelon repair work of combat engineer battalions frequently has been superior to that of general service regiments and engineer aviation battalions. This may be attributed to the fact that combat engineer equipment was issued intermittently. Furthermore, a large percentage of the second and third echelon work on equipment of combat engineer battalions has been accomplished in rest areas prior to and subsequent to their active participation in combat.

MEDICAL SUBJECTS

I. ACTIVITIES OF AN EVACUATION HOSPITAL

Operations.

Aboard Ship—We conducted the hospital on board ship when going from the states and had as high as 130 patients at one time. Likewise on our next trip we conducted the ships' hospital on both of the ships on which our personnel had embarked. A hospital unit when traveling is so frequently looked to for medical help that it should always have a reasonable amount of medical supplies, such as drugs, dressings and instruments with it at all times.

Our laboratory officer had sufficient equipment to do bacteriology for the engineers. Within 24 hours after we landed he had tested the water from various points.

In a period of 10 days we admitted, gave necessary care and evacuated 2,450 patients; and in a total period of 26 hours we broke camp, moved 190 miles, set up camp and had received 300 patients.

Evacuation.

Our evacuation policy changed with the varying circumstances under which we worked. When we were extremely busy we would receive casualties, give necessary treatment and evacuate them all in the space of 48 hours. It was necessary sometimes to evacuate patients in accordance with the news that comes from the front that "we are sending you 500 casualties" but never asking if we had beds to care for them. In such instances, however, we often dismissed patients when our better judgement would have been to keep them for a few more days. Everybody did the very best they could under the circumstances but more beds nearer the front, increasing under stress the bed capacity of a 750-bed evacuation hospital to as high as 1500 beds will go a long way in solving this problem. This, of course, would not decrease the number evacuated eventually but would permit their evacuation under conditions more favorable to the patients. In one campaign we were about 200 miles from the communications zone with highways in only fair condition. We were evacuating by ambulance, by truck, by plane and by train. Evacuation by air is the answer to the evacuation problem.

Personnel.

In our various camps we frequently ran over our listed bed capacity; at one camp we had as high as 1188 patients. With the exception of the litter bearers we had sufficient officer, nurse and enlisted personnel. Under the rapid turnover of patients we experienced, we secured no help from patients as was often the case in station and general hospitals. It was necessary to assign 24 enlisted men for guard duty that is not provided for by our T/O.

Medicine.

Our medical service was surprisingly large having handled 45% of all admissions. This high percentage was due to the fact that we often served as a station hospital. At some time on all fronts conditions might arise requiring that an evacuation hospital do considerable station hospital work. We treated much pneumonia while in the staging area, but very few cases in the theater of operations where the greater percentage of our cases were diarrhea or dysentery. The dysentery was usually of the Flexner type and necessitated about 6 to 10 days hospitalization. This seemed to follow closely infestation with flies. We had relatively little amoebic dysentery even though we did spend the early summer in a known heavy malarial district. Later we did have many malaria cases and often of a most severe type about 20% of our total being Falciparum.

We felt that the use of sulfaguanidine was of great value in the treatment of dysentery cases. While we were having a number of cases among our personnel, we had a standing order that any individual who had a loose bowel movement must go immediately to our dispensary where he would receive 6 grams of sulfaguanidine in one dose to be repeated in 3 hours. This early therapy worked dramatically. As a palliative measure we used bismuth and paregoric.

In our position at the front we treated very little V.D. However, at the times that we were serving as a station hospital we had many cases. We used sulfathiazole in the G.C. cases and lately were using penicillin in the resistant ones. We feel that these resistant cases may be due to inadequate early dosage of the sulfa drug. Our forward dispensary doctors seem to be afraid to give the larger dosages not only of the sulfa drugs but also the barbituates in the anxiety states.

Dermaphttosis.

-We had many cases of epidermophyton infection of the feet. At one census when we had about 700 patients in the hospital there were 34 cases completely inactivated and hospitalized because of epidermophytosis. The soldier says he just can't stop up front to take his shoes off, change his socks and bathe his feet. But if it is going to incapacitate such a high percentage of soldiers with athlete's foot assuredly resulting from such faulty foot care, an enforced routine must be established. It seems to be more extravagant to haul many troops great distances back to the hospital for treatment than it is to stop in the line of march and do a little prophylatic feet drying and washing.

Logistics.

There seems to exist a strong feeling that a 750-bed evacuation hospital is very "immobile", "heavy","troublesome to move", "cumbersome", etc., whereas the 400-bed evacuation hospital is quite mobile. The real facts do not bear this out. A 400-bed unit, in order to move, in addition to its own trucks, must secure 50 trucks from the quartermaster for that purpose. Now, we call for the same 50 trucks and move up half our outfit and take care of 400 patients and then send them back the next day, or later, and bring up the rest of our equipment. With 50 trucks we can move as fast and take care of as many patients as the 400-bed unit and we have about one-fourth more personnel to take care of the additional 350 patients. The best feature of our 750-bed unit is that we furnish a large number of beds economically, both as to basic administrative equipment and personnel.

II. EXTRACTS OF A REPORT ON MEDICAL DEPARTMENT
ACTIVITIES OF A DIVISION DURING AN OPERATION
IN THE SWPA

1. Operations.

a. Practically all of our combat operations were executed in the daytime. The enemy had a technique of night sniping a type of harassing that made night operations unfavorable.

b. Shuttle Scheme. In jungle operations like Island #2, the only available roads were those that were pushed by the bulldozers with our engineer battalion. We made a beachhead and pushed a trail back practically parallel to the front. When each infantry combat team advanced toward the enemy the bulldozers pushed their supply line forward as the combat team progressed. These operations ended about 3:00 in the afternoon and a perimeter defense was laid down around each unit.

Due to unfortunate experiences of earlier troops in that island with their medical units, I thought it was advisable to have our collecting units as well as our clearing company inside the perimeter of defense. Accordingly, I contacted each regimental surgeon and after discussion informed him that I would put a collecting point within his command in the perimeter of defense of that infantry regiment. He could place those men where he wanted them, get them as close as possible to his battalion aid station thereby shortening the litter carry. We had a couple of ambulance jeeps, three or four litter squads and one officer there at all times to operate the collecting point. Then the collecting companies and the clearing company with their kitchens, bivouacked with the service units along the main supply trail that led to the beachhead. They were in the perimeter of defense of the service units. Accordingly, the only ones that were exposed to the sniper fire in daylight hours were the ambulance and jeep drivers who were operating jeeps as ambulances. I feel that this cut down our casualties in the medical department considerably and expedited the evacuation because it kept the litter haul as short as possible and kept all of our medical units inside the perimeter of an infantry outfit.

The area of a perimeter varied with the operation of the regiment. First, you'll have to visualize that there were only two infantry battalions, with each one of these infantry regiments; the third battalion of the regiment and third battalion of another regiment were separated from their parent units. They were to establish a road block on a trail on one side of Island #2. At the same time we were approaching a village from the other side of the island. The harbor was the same harbor that the enemy used in bringing their supplies and men from other islands. With those two battalions of infantry, if there were only one in the line and one in reserve, which happens sometimes, I would say roughly that 50 to 75 yards was the diameter of their perimeter. However, if they were spread out in a line, that practically doubled it in one direction and made it less in the other. It was flexible and varied according to the width of the front which the combat team had to cover. Our battalion aid stations were practically in the line. As a matter of fact our division headquarters was only about 300 to 400 yards from the line; and the regimental headquarters anywhere from 100 to 50 yards from the front line, so you see the battalion aid station was right up with the fighting troops. They were in foxholes. It was really a series of emplacements which were used to get our infantry up to where they could polish off the enemy who were pretty well dug in. The jungle prevented extensive operations. You couldn't deploy in text-book fashion and fight according to ordinary infantry tactics. I would say that it was nearly like our American Colonial Indian fighting, from tree-to-tree with the exception that the enemy was using more lethal weapons and probably digging more holes to defend themselves from our weapons. The addition of artillery on our side was a godsend to us and the lack of it on the enemy side aided us materially.

2. Medical Situations:

      The prevailing disease was malaria. It was more noticeable
in the Regimental combat team of another division than it was in our combat
teams because they had been in the malaria zone from two to three months
longer than our units. They had seen action at Island #1 and probable
their resistance was lower. I don't think it was due to any lack of discipline
because they were an excellent organization and well commanded, but they did
have a higher malaria rate than our division. Over two-thirds of their
non-battle casualties, while only roughly one-fifth of our non-battle casualties, were malaria cases, which is quite a striking difference. As a
control measure we used the malaria control unit, which I have mentioned
before, to check on the use of repellents, the clothing of the soldiers and
atabrine discipline all the time in addition to checking drainage, oiling
pools and filling ruts. They were under the supervision of the Medical
Inspector and the Division Surgeon. Atabrine descipline out of combat was
fairly simple. We had each mess checked by a non-commissioned officer under
the supervision of an officer so that everyone that ate at that mess was
checked on paper when he took his atabrine. We did this throughout the
Division when we moved from another island to Island #1. In combat that
responsibility broke down, but we provided each group of four enlisted men
with an improvised jungle kit. Since the regulation Army Jungle Kit was
not available to us, we made up these improvised kits, using the Planter's
Peanut Cans, available in great number in which the troops had just received
a large issue of cigarettes. This peanut can was about 3 inches in diameter
and about $2\frac{1}{2}$ inches deep. We had each Battalion Surgeon make up kits for
his outfit, putting a dozen calcium hypochlorite tubes (1/2 gram size),
two dozen atabrine tablets (gr. $1\frac{1}{2}$), band aids, 1 roller bandage, 1 - 1" roll
adhesive, four iodine swabs and 2 dozen salt tablets (gr. 10) in each can.
A directive was issued which reached every man in the division stating how
each item was used and that the supply would be replenished on request at
the Battalion Aid Station. Unfortunately halazone tablets for water purifica-
tion were not available. Accordingly, in the directive on the use of the
jungle kit, we informed them how to use calcium hypochlorite in the mess cup
to make water safe for drinking purposes. The use of this kit, atabrine
discipline, clothing discipline (keeping arms and legs covered in early morning and late afternoon), bed nets and constant vigilance in destroying mosquito breeding places--all assisted in keeping our malaria rate so amazingly
low, but the fundamental thing was the cooperative, understanding leadership
of the Commanding General which pervaded the entire division and made the
practice of sound medical and sanitary policies not only possible but mandatory.

      We had some mild dysenteries but nothing that was really
alarming. It was a dysentery, however, because we had several instances of
bloody mucous stools. However, I think the greater part of them stayed on
duty because only a very few reached our clearing station. We had no dengue.
There was a lot of skin infection which is quite common in the tropics. I
mean the trichophytosis, or the ringworm type of infection. This increased
throughout the combat until we returned to Island #1 when practically 50%
of our casualties were skin cases. When we reached our Island #1 rest area,
they had epidermophytosis of either the feet, legs, groin, hands or sometimes
the entire body was involved. There were, of course, a lot of secondary
infections. I'm not positive as to the cause. Stitt mentions in his
Tropical Diseases that there are a vast number of skin infesting fungi that

prevail in the troops which really haven't been classified yet. It didn't seem as severe as our so-called "athlete's foot" or ringworm infections that we have in this country but they were severe enough to make casualties out of men, especially when they wore dirty clothing for a couple of weeks and couldn't take a bath. Such a situation prevailed during the operation.

III. EVACUATION OF WOUNDED PERSONNEL

General. Successful and rapid evacuation of wounded depends upon the following: (1) Aggressiveness of unit surgeons in keeping personnel and unit installations well forward. (2) Close coordination and contact between the division surgeon and surgeons of subordinate units. (3) The establishment of ambulance loading points along the axis of advance.

IV. EXTRACTS OF AN OPERATION REPORT

The medical requirements of the division for this operation were considered adequately met by the proposed attachment of two (2) portable surgical hospitals and two (2) field hospitals. The requested attachments were met only in part, there being attached to the division, a portable surgical hospital and a field hospital. The jungle kit, M-2 (medical supply catalog) was procured and issued as a medical aid container replacing the packet, first aid, per individual. This container was also to carry salt tablets, insect powder and chap-sticks.

Evacuation:

a. Prior to Embarkation: All medical department ¼-ton trucks were equipped with ambulance litter frames enabling each to evacuate four litter and one ambulatory patient at a time.

b. Embarkation: All medical personnel, equipment and supplies were combat loaded. This put in position to be unloaded with each infantry battalion the following:

The battalion medical section	2 officers and 32 enlisted men.
Collecting platoon of medical battalion	1 officer and 28 enlisted men.
Engineer shore party medical detachment	1 officer and 5 enlisted men.

The clearing company was loaded in two separate platoons, each on separate ships and each capable of functioning separately. The portable surgical hospital was loaded with the platoon which was to be initially committed. The field hospital was loaded by hospitalization units, each of the three hospitalization units capable of operating separately as a clearing station or as a hospitalization unit in support of the battalion landing team with which it was loaded. All equipment and supplies were priority loaded. That equipment immediately necessary for the collecting platoons was loaded in the ¼-ton trucks which were unloaded on an early priority. The equipment necessary for the initial set-up of each platoon of the clearing company and each hospitalization unit of the field hospital was loaded on 2 - 2½-ton trucks which were to be disembarked with the personnel.

c. Operations Ashore: The clearing company with the portable surgical hospital set up its initial station on the southern part of the island in a small village of partially wrecked houses on 19 June 1944 and operated there until 23 June 1944 when the field hospital took over the installation and patients, the clearing company displacing forward to furnish close support to the combat elements which were advancing up (north) the island. During the entire operation from 17 June till 12 July 1944 the portable surgical hospital was employed with the clearing station or the field hospital, wherever necessity required. Supplies and equipment during the initial phases came ashore on the several beaches already in use by two marine divisions. This resulted in some confusion, much time being spent locating equipment and supplies and the loss of some of it.

The collecting companies which had been attached to their respective RCT's and landed with the BLT's as platoons were, after the initial phase line was reached, returned to the control of the medical battalion and functioned thenceforth in the conventional pattern of collecting stations supporting a regimental zone of action. Evacuation from the front was thru the collecting stations to the clearing station, the field hospital, and from there to hospital ships, transport or airplane. This procedure was in operation by 20 June 1944 and operated smoothly. The use of the frame-equipped $\frac{1}{4}$-ton truck as an ambulance from the front lines back as far as the hospital worked very satisfactorily. There was no appreciable evacuation lag throughout the evacuation chain. Three sanitary squads of one (1) officer and ten (10) enlisted men each were formed from the collecting companies of the medical battalion and used to spray friendly and enemy dead with sodium arsenite. This procedure was satisfactory and aided materially in the sanitation of the area. The use of sodium arsenite in straddle trenches and garbage pits also helped the fly problem.

Supply:

Each medical unit carried organically a one day reserve of strategic items such as plasma, morphine syrettes and first aid dressings both large and small. The clearing company carried a three day reserve and the field hospital a ten day reserve. For this reason resupply was not made necessary for at least three days by which time the division medical supply was in position to function from dumps ashore.

The automatic exchange and issue of medical supplies functioned satisfactorily. The only source of difficulty was the rapid loss of litters and blankets occasioned by a breakdown in exchange. Whether this occurred at the beach or on the field will never actually be determined, however, litters became quickly a critical item without any source of resupply. During the later phases of the operation litters were salvaged from the cemeteries, cleaned up and reissued.

Comments and Recommendations:

1. Supply.

The palletization of medical supplies has proven this procedure most satisfactory and should become standard practice. The items used may vary in different situations but changes can be readily effected to meet these conditions.

2. Equipment:

It has been noted that man hours are wasted in unloading dual purpose $\frac{1}{4}$-ton trucks. This could be remedied by using a $\frac{1}{4}$-ton trailer for packing medical equipment. This would permit unloading only such supplies as are required, utilizing the truck itself as an ambulance without interfering with the equipment of the station.

3. Evacuation.

a. The clearing station should not be expanded to perform the functions of hospitalization. It becomes less mobile because of extra equipment and is tied down because of post-operative patients who cannot be moved.

b. Local security must be provided by combat agencies or the medical units must be reinforced with defense platoons.

Comments: On Specific Questions (Consensus of Opinion).

1. All medical installations were established as close to trails and exit roads as was commensurate with the tactical situation. For the most part the medical installations were included in the perimeter of the organization supported by them, e.g., the battalion aid stations were usually part of the battalion command post, the collecting stations with the regimental command post and as a result were on the axis of communication which was also the natural line of drift and in close proximity to critical points.

Summary:

a. Netting for enclosure of kitchens, mess halls and latrines should be an item of issue for future operations.

b. Attempt should be made to deliver prefabricated latrines and drums to units in the field at the earliest possible moment.

Summary of Psychiatric Casualties:

a. Admissions occurred primarily in young individuals.

b. Treatment in forward areas with sedation and psychotherapy is apparently the method of choice.

c. Attempts to screen out the potential psychiatric casualty when in garrison has paid dividends.

d. Psychiatric lectures, as prescribed by TB #12, to all medical officers of the division, proved beneficial.

Suggestions and Recommendations for Future Operations:

1. The personnel of a medical battalion is trained to perform medical duties only. This personnel is inadequate under the present T/O to perform other than medical duties.

2. On several occasions tank units moved into the areas adjacent to collecting company sites and soon thereafter these areas became the subject of enemy bombing or shelling. It is definitely felt that these tanks drew the shell fire which caused the death of three of our enlisted men and the injury of several others. It is suggested that tactical units do not pick areas near medical installations.

3. It is also suggested that clearing company personnel not be used for evacuating the clearing company thereby cutting down much needed personnel.

4. It has been the policy of this battalion to pick up all ordnance material at the collecting companies and clearing company. It is suggested that each collecting company and the clearing company be visited each day by ordnance for the purpose of removing salvage material. The quartermaster should also make daily visits to pick up their salvage.

Comments:

For security during the operation the company always moved within the regimental perimeter.

Except for unusual conditions the medical vehicles were adequate for evacuation. However, it's rather a cumbersome task to move equipment and personnel during combat when most of the vehicles are in use evacuating casualties either from the aid station to the collecting station or from the collecting station to the clearing station.

The use of medical personnel for a sanitary detail is a waste of trained men.

Suggestions and Criticisms:

1. Litter squads assisting battalion aid should be given adequate guards and guides when they go forward.

2. Debarkation schedules should have the collecting platoons in the last wave rather than priority boats. The first platoon in priority boats lost contact with their battalion aid station as a result of landing late.

3. Litters and blankets should be available for front line use at all times even at the expense of clearing company and station hospitals. In my opinion, it is more important to move patients from the front lines than it is to evacuate them back from clearing company or from hospitals (unit).

Resume:

1. The present disposal of a collecting company in time of action is the most practical method of function. This gives the collecting company's commanding officer an opportunity to make a correct appraisal of evacuation needs. On numerous occasions, anxious demands were made by various surgeons. If personnel of this company had been disposed as desired on several occasions the efficiency of this unit would have been impaired.

2. In a majority of instances there was very little cover for the station, personnel or patients. Only at one time did we set up a tent during the day to protect the patients from the sun. Most of the time we worked in the open and were not troubled by the rain.

3. Most of the time there was contact by vehicle with each battalion aid station. Likewise, we had two liaison men with each battalion aid station during the active operation.

Comments and Remarks:

1. During the combat some 100 whole blood transfusions were given in the clearing station. Of this, 60 to 75% of the clearing company personnel donated the blood. The last two weeks of combat it became necessary to use donors furnished by the division.

2. Sites and Security: The clearing station was at all times set up near the main highways to facilitate evacuation of patients from forward areas. Cover and concealment and dispersion were utilized whenever possible and when available. On several occasions the clearing station was placed too far forward and on one occasion set up in an area that was known to be under enemy artillery fire prior to the set up of station. The clearing station that is pinned down by small arms or artillery fire is of no value to anyone. In all this time the clearing station had to provide for their own local security and very frequently it consisted of men who had worked all day in the station and then would go on guard at night.

3. Supply: In the frequent movement of a great deal of equipment, some very heavy, rendering medical care to a large number of casualties, giving blood for blood transfusions for a large number of casualties, providing local security, evacuating large numbers of casualties, wounded civilians, prisoners-of-war and the dead, the clearing company found itself oversupplied with equipment and undersupplied with personnel.

The clearing station was so overburdened with supplies and equipment that they were well nigh immobilized. It became necessary to leave most of their equipment and supplies in a dump where they drew their supplies as needed.

Only the combat-loaded equipment on vehicles needs be duplicated for both platoons. X-ray and orthopedic tables are not needed for a clearing station. Duplication of heavy electrical equipment is not needed. Canvas, cots, mosquito nets, frames and blankets for no more than 200 patients should be carried. Simple oxygen masks with valve and gauge are superior to Boothby Lovelace apparatus.

Recommendations:

1. Evacuation of clearing station was inadequate and should be done by corps troops.

2. Clearing station personnel be left with station and not detached to other units. Two vehicles with drivers were detached soon after landing on island.

3. Definite personnel be assigned to pick up equipment on beach before it is stolen or lost.

4. Many casualties were evacuated to clearing station when their wounds were superficial and could easily have been handled at battalion aid station. Syphilitic patients were evacuated to clearing station for their routine treatment during the peak of combat when the station was vigorously engaged in treating many battle casualties. If syphilitic troops are in combat units they should be the type able to do without treatment during the combat period.

Professional Experience during operation from 20 June - 10 July 1944 inclusive:

1. The provision of definitive surgical care in the zone of combat is fraught with extreme difficulty. To utilize properly a group equipped to furnish such care involves integration of numerous factors which are chron- ically conflicting. The complexity of the problem is admitted; nevertheless, it is asserted that there is a tendency among medical officers caught in the toils of tactics to minimize unduly some of the basic professional principles. This plea for a more professional point of view is therefore entered. Except when major advances or withdrawals of the fighting line occur which obviously force station movement it is urged that change of station be accomplished only when indicated by professional need. When the journey from the lines becomes so long or arduous that it in itself is productive of surgical shock movement becomes mandatory on medical grounds. Likewise, when the arrival of the wounded is so delayed that wounds are no longer amenable to surgical attack, change of station is essential for the fulfillment of the mission. It is strongly urged that in the selection of station location every effort be held for at least a few days of postoperative care. The value of major surgical intervention is extremely dubious if rest and post- operative attention cannot be furnished as has already been mentioned.

2. Triage, as stated in various articles and reports dealing with military medical subjects, presents a difficult problem. To keep several operating teams functioning continuously requires a competent officer selecting the cases. His efforts must be, and were supplemented by those of the operating surgeons. As experience accumulated, most medical officers acquired some knowledge of triage and although there were periods which were somewhat chaotic when large numbers of casualties appeared simultan- eously the sorting for the most part was well done.

3. The shock problem is always with us in military surgery. Plasma has greatly altered the complexion for the better and justly deserves the numerous accolades administered by enthusiastic literature. It is not, however, the sole answer and has not displaced the need for whole blood in cases of hemorrhage nor the necessity for the crystalloid fluids in succes- sion in some cases. It was injected simultaneously in more than one vein in some instances. Twice the intrasternal route was employed but our equipment was not satisfactory for this maneuver. It would have been applicable several times had the equipment been suitable. Plasma was used during an operation frequently. A number of urgent cases can be operated while receiving plasma which could not otherwise receive treatment.

4. In our experience the majority of the wounded are in a state of rather serious dehydration. Most of them perspired extremely freely during combat. Often they have had access to water in minimal amounts which appear to have been unequal to their fluid loss. Practically all are in nearly as much need of crystalloid as of colloid replacement. If the theory that colloids in the blood stream draw fluids out of the tissues is correct it becomes hard to imagine how this mechanism can operate in the presence of dehydration without aggravating this condition, if indeed this osmosis is functional at all. This thesis has been mentioned in the literature. It was our custom to administer one to two thousand cc of crystalloid fluids to serious cases in addition to such quantity of colloidal fluid as proved essential. The general condition improved more than when plasma alone was given.

The preparation of the hands of the operator and assistants was crude. The shortage of water forced this upon us. It was necessary to use a hand basin and scrub brush, scrubbing under running water constituted too prodigal a use of this substance. Following the soap and water scrub the hands and arms were rinsed in 1/1000 bichloride of mercury solution. The conclusion of the preparation consisted in an alcohol rinse. For the most part, gloves were put on dry but some of us preferred the wet technique and donned the gloves with bichloride in them. There has been a strong tendency in recent years to abandon antiseptics as part of the operative toilet. The wisdom of this change is so questionable in the minds of some of us as seen under the conditions of civilian practice. When confronted with the unavoidable filth of field conditions in the theater of action, antisepsis necessarily supersedes asepsis and antiseptics applied to the hands of the surgeon are no longer mere refinement but a dire need. The revival of the one time frequently used method of applying chloride of lime paste to the forearms and hands would be desirable.

6. Preparation of the patient was a difficult problem since such a large number of severe wounds had to be prepared by the operator on the table and under anesthesia. This prolonged the period of anesthesia and also diminished the productivity of an operating team. Nevertheless no other satisfactory solution presented itself.

7. Sodium pentothal was used for practically all cases save laparotomies which were performed under open drop ether. In the main it was highly satisfactory from the standpoint of operator and patient. Shock did not appear to be increased. Relaxation was reasonably good. Respiration was not unduly depressed except in unusual instances ordinarily resulting from too rapid administration even though the anesthetic was for the most part given by enlisted men. There were no postoperative complications directly attributed to sodium pentothal. Spinal, employing procaine, was used in a few cases of lower leg injury who were not in shock. Undoubtedly it would have found somewhat wider application if pentothal had not been as successful.

8. Debridement consistuted the most frequently employed procedure. In many instances it was the only treatment. In others it was a preface to more formidable undertakings. Rarely, if ever, did it assume the more refined forms of wounds excision. The nature of the wounds, so often involving vital structures, the crudity of the operative toilet and the co-existence of shock in many instances, all these factors combined to prevent the more meticulous

approach. In the early stages of our work there was a tendency toward con-
servatism which expressed itself in an effort to avoid sacrifice of tissue.
This was good insofar as it resulted in preservation of skin. But when this
meant insufficient exposure to permit removal of all dead muscle tissue the
evil was obvious. This was forcibly brought to our attention by the appear-
ance of a few cases of anaerobic infection some of which were probably less
dangerous varieties such as anaerobic streptococcus but a few of which were
clinically frank instances of gas gangrene, probably caused by the more
dangerous anaerobes such as B. Welchii; after encountering these, our technique became more radical. Skin can be and was preserved. Exposure sufficient
to allow adequate operation and ample admittance of air was gained by making
linear incisions from the wound. This practice has been suggested in the
literature and we heartily endorse this procedure as a method of value.
Muscle tissue must be sacrificed until free bleeding, healthy color and normal
contractility that all devitalize tissue is gone. Fascia when loose and torn
is removed. Detached fragments of shattered bone were plucked out of the
wounds, however, when fastened by pericateum to grossly uninjured bone, or
when attached to a fair size segiment of vital muscle the fragments were not
disturbed unless grossly contaminated. Important structures such as nerves,
tendons and blood vessels were spared whenever possible which of course is
practically universal custom.

9. Maxillo-facial injuries were definitely treated in only a few instances where a lessened volume of casualty flow permitted. Debridement in
these instances was sparingly and conservatively performed. Following
destructive surgical treatment, suture was accomplished by figure of eight
stitches in order to obtain approximation of the deeper tissues. Drainage
with a rubber hose was employed in one instance. In the cases treated,
wiring of the teeth was done. In one instance the maxilla was externally
wired to a skull cap of plaster.

10. Numerous sucking wounds of the chest were seen. It was our practice
to close these tightly following debridement. Tension pneumothorax occurred
in only one subsequent to closure while the patient was under our care. A
small cathetar was treaded into the chest through a trocar and sewed to the
skin with condom valve attached to its outer end. The relief was dramatic.
Open thoracotomy was not attempted. Insufficient time, inadequate equipment
and lack of trained personnel all counsel against such an undertaking.
Possibly there may be exceptions where such a procedure would be justified
but we did not see any. In a few instances it is necessary to aspirate
massive hemothorax to ease labored respiration but most of these are best
left alone.

11. Injuries of large blood vessels are often not obvious. It was
astonishing to see three still alive in which the subclavion artery had
been severed by the passage of a missile through the shoulder. There was no
active hemorrhage nor any hemotoma in these instances on their arrival at
our station. Injuries to blood vessels of the extremities generally arrive
with a tourniquet applied. Sometimes no hemorrhage ensued when this was
removed although this was not the rule. The body mechanisms to control
hemorrhage are more effectual than some of us had heretofore believed. The
initial violent hemorrhage is of course, productive of profound shock, with
associated lowering of the blood pressure so that clotting occurs. In
addition, in the case of arteries, an astounding marked vasco-constriction

ensues. Treatment in the majority of cases consists of litigation since the damage to the vessel is usually so marked as to obviate any attempt at suture. The advice given in guides to therapy for medical officer (p 33 - 50) TM 8-210 is eminently valuable. The writer opines that all operating surgeons should be advised to familiarize themselves with this excellent reference. In cases such as the three severed subclavian arteries the counsel to approach the artery through the incision of election above the wound was apropos and spared enormous technical difficulty and possibly the life of the patient.. In two of these three cases with suspected injury to the vessels incision was made above the clavicle. The artery was identified and tape placed around it. The wound was then explored to ascertain the extent of the damage to the vessels. The resultant hemorrhage was easily controlled. When it was discovered that the vessel was damaged beyond repair, ligation with heavy silk was performed in the wound and at the point of election. Transaction of the vessels in the elective wound was accomplished after ligation above and below. The above cases were outlined in some detail since they illustrate the utility of exposure of vessels above the wound prior to exploration of a wound. This principle finds its greatest application in situations where the tourniquet cannot be employed but may also have value under other circumstances. In our experience we also encountered the necessity of ligating the femoral artery and vein at various levels the poplitical artery and other vessels of lesser size. It impressed us as being an important problem where diagnosis is not always easy and where proper treatment may be technically difficult.

12. In our experience wounds of the abdomen fully merited the gloomy prognosis which they have always had. The shock associated with them is ordinarily profound. Nevertheless, with the aid of plasma, it is remarkable how formidable a technical procedure they will withstand. In approaching these cases we uniformly employed ample right and left rectus incisions which were converted to L or T incisions without hesitation if further exposure was needed. Upon opening the abdomen, the damage to the viscera appeared out of all proportion to the oft times relatively innocuous looking external wounds. Usually several perforations of the small gut were discovered. Frequently wounds of the liver and large gut were co-existent, wounds of the small intestine were closed with interrupted catgut stitches in such a manner that a resulting sature line was transverse to the long axis of the bowel. Resection was not required in our series. Wounds of the large intentine were all exteriorized over a glass or rubber tube thru stab wounds. The more finished Mickulicz procedure was not employed since even the small amount of extra time necessary was begrudged. In a few cases where the T incision was employed exteriorization was done thru one corner of the incision. Since this is technically undesirable it was avoided wherever possible. Liver bleeding was controlled by diverse means according to its gravity. In the simplier instances figure of eight stitches were used. In others, packs of muscle or mental tissues were employed. Complete abdominal exploration is necessary and was done in all cases where the nature of the injury made it very clear that this was not needed. Only a few wounds of the urinary bladder were seen. These were treated by closure of abdominal incisions ordinarily done by interrupted heavy silk stitches including all layers. In other instances layer closure was done with catgut the remaining layers being approximated by interrupted heavy silk stitches incorporating all layers down to the peritoneum.

13. During the early days of our experience we employed a number of circular casts in fractures of upper and lower extremities. Soon the wisdom of this procedure became doubtful. Toward the end we tended to use molded plaster splints more frequently. We had intended to bivalve all circular casts before they left our station but a number were moved without this having been done. In order to avoid this occurrence and because of the fear of anaerobic infections we gradually adopted the molded plaster splint. No unpadded plaster casts or splint were employed. No pins nor plates were used in treating fractures, there were, however, a few instances where their use would have been advantageous since no other way of avoiding shortening of fractured limbs is conceivable. In the main sagacity of the directive condemning the use of pins and plates was apparent. All the fractures which were observed were compounded and grossly contaminated. One does not need the gift of prophecy to predict infection with profuse drainage as the probable fate of the majority of these wounds. Nevertheless, it can be deplored that we are deprived of these valuable methods of treatment. Although it is impossible, without being able to follow the cases to appraise the so called tobruk splint, we opined it unsatisfactory. The application of the device is time consuming. The degree of force of traction is probably insufficient. It has the advantage of conveying the impression that the principle of traction has been invoked. It is less cumbersome than a hip spica. The answer to the problem of limb shortening probably lies in the tobruk splint or a modification thereof. It surely would be found therein if some compound to insure adherence of tape to skin could be made available.

Location of Station:

On the basis of our experience it is felt that this unit will function most efficiently when used to augment the surgical personnel of a larger unit in a location far enough behind the front lines that uninterrupted postoperative care may be given abdominal and chest cases for at least 5 to 10 days. If tactical necessity dictates the transfer of this unit to an area within range of enemy fire and local terrain does not offer defilade and concealment it is recommended that artificial dugouts be constructed for the unit. Our experience has repeatedly demonstrated the fact that employment of this unit too far forward defeats its purpose.

V. SCRUB-TYPHUS

Theater Surgeon, March 1944.

The prediction as to the danger of scrub-typhus in any new area is at present based only upon the generality that the foci are commonly found in kunai grassland. It appears probable also that areas with a high growth of grass sufficient to maintain moisture about the roots is another factor in the prevalence of the scrub-typhus sector.

The incubation period was certain to be between 10 and 17 days with the probability that the incubation period was 11 or 12 days.

The protective measures to be taken against this disease are:

1. Areas will, whenever possible, be cleared by cutting and burning of kunai grass and brushing out of jungle prior to arrival of troops for bivouac or staging therein.

2. Men working in kunai grass will be fully clothed, wearing leggins and with rolled-down sleeves. Men will avoid sitting or lying on the ground especially in kunai patches on stumps or on fallen tree trunks.

3. Whenever possible, on completion of work in kunai grass and brush, men will bathe at once soaping the entire body.

4. Kunai grass will not be used for mattresses or pillows.

5. Whenever possible, troops will sleep on jungle hammocks, cots or on native type beds constructed of saplings and supported about two feet from the ground on crotched posts and crossbars.

6. Such measures as may be possible will be taken to exterminate rats and other rodents.

VI. ARMY NOTES

AGF Board, January 1944.

Medical units are being employed essentially in the capacity for which organized. Due to the specialized nature of amphibious operations in this theater, there are inevitable variations in the details of employment in specific cases but none to justify changes except as noted below.

The conventional medical battalion, if strengthened by the addition of a third medical platoon to the clearing company, can meet all requirements made on it. There seems to be no need for a new type medical battalion.

As far as can be judged on the basis of observation in rear areas and a limited amount of battle experience, division medical units appear to be well trained tactically and technically. Evacuation hospitals, when they have a competent commanding officer, arrive well trained; without such commanding officers they appear poorly disciplined and trained.

Divisional non-medical units are properly trained in first aid and sanitation; other units usually are not.

Anti-malaria discipline is difficult to enforce in newly-arrived units as well as in old ones. The simple requirement to wear shirts with sleeves unrolled and buttoned is very frequently violated. A gratifying exception was noted by an AGF Board member in the troops of one operation. In a second operation another Board member observed a very high percentage of the men stripped to the waist at all times of the day; questioning disclosed that many men accepted malaria as something like battle wounds or death - one gets it if his number is up.

Cover and concealment of medical installations is used when feasible. In one operation available space for clearing and shore evacuation stations

made necessary their location in immediate proximity to proper military targets
for enemy artillery or aviation. It is estimated that similar conditions
will be encountered in future operations.

In the open the cross is used. In one operation a member of the AGF
Board saw an unconcealed and marked hospital bombed with several casualties,
and considerable property damage. Repeated inquiry has disclosed no authentic
instance in which the Japanese have honored the cross.

The 750-bed evacuation hospital would be needed for certain task forces,
where otherwise two 400-bed hospitals would be required. These units can
serve every need which might arise in a field army, and, aside from a
convalescent hospital, no other type of hospital is necessary.

In advance of the evacuation hospital, no surgery should ordinarily
be attempted except affecting hemostatis, dressing wounds, splinting fractures,
treating surgical shock and similar emergency measures. A Board member
saw a medical officer use a considerable array of surgical instruments on
a severe abdominal wound within 100 yards of the enemy in an advance.

Such operations as have been undertaken to date have been amphibious
and of necessity have been carried out by task forces. All medical units
are, therefore, attached to the force and come under the control of the task
force surgeon.

Experience to date has indicated no essential changes are necessary in
equipment.

Directional signs habitually are used to mark routes to medical installations.

Present communication means for medical installations are satisfactory;
no need for radio is foreseen.

No difficulty in the replacement of critical items has developed so far.

The maintenance and repair of medical equipment in advance areas has
been poor. In these areas, equipment needing repair is turned over to
medical supply for return to the rear.

Authorized transportation of medical units has been adequate in all
cases. Distances ashore are short and rarely can all transportation
be taken in amphibious operations until the late stages. Shuttling is the
rule. In transporting casualties it is necessary at times to use borrowed
vehicles.

No changes in assigned transportation of medical units are deemed
essential.

A mobile operating room is not needed by clearing companies. Surgery
should not be done except by evacuation hospitals.

Our standard ambulance surpasses the jeep in every respect.

Members of the AGF Board observed the use of the jeep ambulance on two operations with the following comments:

1st Operation

A member of the Board saw wounded transported in 3/4-ton truck ambulances and in $2\frac{1}{2}$-ton trucks. He heard on good authority that some wounded had been evacuated by a returning amphibious tractor which had accompanied the leading assault troops in a tank role. The $\frac{1}{4}$-ton truck ambulances were very rough but they were the first wheeled vehicles which were able to negotiate the mud and slope to the main ridge of the peninsula. As a result, it appeared that they were used almost exclusively on D-day. They continued to be popular, for on D $\neq$ 14, a medical unit was requested to leave its three $\frac{1}{4}$-ton vehicles when it returned to its base to prepare for another operation. However, after D-day the only means of transportation of wounded, which the Board member saw, was $2\frac{1}{2}$-ton trucks. They were operating principally forward of the aid stations.

Due to the terrain, the $\frac{1}{4}$-ton ambulances provided more mobility than any other vehicle. The shorter wheelbase and smaller turning radius of the $\frac{1}{4}$-ton permitted it to avoid obstacles which larger vehicles would have to pass over. Even after a road was built the $\frac{1}{4}$-ton trucks were capable of more movement than other vehicles through the jungle growth beyond and to either side of the road.

The member of the board did not see standard ambulances used but was told that they were being utilized. In all evacuation it appeared that the most available transportation was used in an effort to speed the wounded to the rear. All of the vehicles which were transporting wounded, which the member of the board saw, were most carefully driven.

The litter racks on the $\frac{1}{4}$-ton ambulances appeared to have been improvised. They caused the litters to extend quite far to the rear thus increasing the severity of jolts. For this reason it would appear that whenever terrain conditions permit the standard ambulance or the $2\frac{1}{2}$-ton truck should be used.

2nd Operation.

$\frac{1}{4}$-ton trucks in considerable numbers were used to supplement the standard ambulances which were at times inadequate to handle the number of casualties. Casualties could not have been loaded nearly as far forward on the standard ambulance as on the jeep.

The observer accompanied one of several $2\frac{1}{2}$-ton trucks, a trip requiring about four hours for a distance of about five miles, mostly under red alert conditions, on a very dark night. The $2\frac{1}{2}$-ton trucks negotiated two very deep mud passages where several jeeps had to be towed by tractors. The $2\frac{1}{2}$ ton truck was able to ford crossings too deep for the jeep. It definitely appeared that the jeep ambulance was less comfortable than the standard ambulance or $2\frac{1}{2}$-ton truck. The short wheel base and unavoidably high mounting of stretchers in the jeep would appear to make this the case under usual forward area road conditions.

SIGNAL SUBJECTS

I. RADIO EQUIPMENT

Communication by means of SCR 536's had been established from the command post on a destroyer to the unit which landed on a nearby island to the commanding officer of the assault wave and to the commanding officer of the reserve as soon as radio silence was broken. He also reported the maintenance of this net until all of the stations were ashore.

The task force signal officer was forced to set up his SCR-299 (for communication with army headquarters) initially in a low area near the beach because of inability of the vehicles to negotiate mud and the slope to the main ridge. When a trail through the mud and up the slope had been slightly improved and a tractor became available to assist he moved into a position just north of the crest of the ridge. (Individuals and small groups of the enemy were known to be in the jungle about 400 yards from the crest). From that position he still could not gain communication. He moved the set to the crest and installed a special aerial above the cocoanut trees. He sent and received acknowledgment of a message to army headquarters in the early evening.

Radio personnel of the division and task force headquarters were well-trained and all sets were tested and worked on D-2. (These units were aboard ships from the afternoon of D-2 until the landing, so testing on D-1 was impracticable). All sets were wrapped in pouches or inclosed in waterproof bags while in transit. Three boxes of K ration were placed in a waterproof bag on the morning of D-2. When opened in the early evening of D, considerable moisture had condensed inside the bag .

Remaining units of the task force embarked on D-1. Therefore, their set would be tested and wrapped early that day in dry weather.

The member of the board was informed by the army signal officer that they had no reliable communication with the command post station until sometime on D ≠ 1. All messages which they received from that source until early on D ≠ 1 had to be sent over the air support net in order to insure receipt. Later the air support communication failed and for a short period their communications were sent over the command net.

The artillery commander stated to the member of the board that his radios had worked consistently. He ascribed this to the fact that his organization dried out their radios daily by placing them in a box with a lighted lantern. He had one enlisted man who did nothing but inspect radios daily, on location, fix them up for drying and make any adjustments or repairs necessary.

II. SIGNAL EQUIPMENT

Troops are equipped with panel AP-50. No use for them was found in this operation. No use of panels was observed although had occasion for their use arisen after D-3 the terrain and vegetation would have permitted their use. On D and D-1 accidentally and partially displayed panels might have served to attract enemy air attention.

Departures from standard maintenance procedure are normal rather than exceptional. Special preventive maintenance must be observed. All equipment, distances and mode of travel between units and bases preclude normal echelons of maintenance. Lower units must provide some higher echelons of maintenance at all times.

An all-magneto type switchboard presents a critical problem in this theater because of maintaining local telephone batteries. It is the opinion of the army signal officer that common battery switchboard should be used at all headquarters from division on up. Maintaining local batteries is a tremendous problem, because humidity and heat lower their life about 50%.

There is no need for semi-mobile operation of the corps switchboard in this theater. A truck set up for use as a switchboard would preclude its use for carrying other cargo, and the CP is not expected ever to move hurriedly.

Radio stations must always be remote-controlled. The distance transmitters should be placed away from the receivers varies inversely with the distance from troops in contact - one-half to one mile in forward areas, 200 to 300 yards where air attack is seldom experienced.

Most failures in equipment were due to humidity, salt water immersion, or just plain carelessness. The army signal officer instituted a plan of preventive maintenance which somewhat reduces the mortality in equipment. Condensers, resistors, coils and contacts are the principal items which fail. A weekly check of all equipment in use or in storage will usually result in keeping these items dry and clean. In landing operations the salt and humid atmosphere and the all pervading splash and spray of tropical downpours indicates the need of a controlled heat source for field drying and maintaining a workable degree of dryness. It is possible that low-temperature heaters similar to the pocket warmers used by sportsmen, or hot water bottle substitute, might be satisfactory.

Training received in maneuvers has been valuable in that units have had some experience in setting up and operating CPs. There, the similarity between maneuver and combat conditions (in this theater) ceases. No one who has not experienced the setting up and maintaining of a communication system in pouring rains, hacking out right-of-way for wire lines, can imagine the difficulties. The possible routes of wire lines for the early and vital days of the operation were along a narrow strip of beach backed by swamps, or along narrow passages through swamps, impassable for any practicable use by foot or vehicle of any type. What had been a heavy forest had been reduced to chaos by bombing and shelling. On this narrow beach was very heavy activity of bulldozers, tractors, tanks, amphibious tractors, other heavy vehicles, and troops having immediate need to establish supply dumps and artillery positions wherever space could be found. Wire lines in many stretches simply had to follow the coast track. The activities of amphibious tractors repeatedly broke wires where it was impossible to string them overhead in the time available. Repeated instances of excellent telephone communication to forward artillery observers with assault units, to heavy weapons units, and between forward command posts attested to the persistant hard work and resourcefulness of communication personnel. The wire W-110 showed remarkable ability to stand up under rough usage.

REPORT ON CIC IN ITALY

The purposes of CIC are counter-espionage, counter-sabotage and counter-subversion. Each corps and division has attached a CIC team to carry our this work within the corps and division sectors. The division team is responsible for their zone of operation back to the division rear boundary. The corps team covers the area behind the division rear boundary, back to the corps rear boundary, assists the division team whenever it requires assistance and sets up informants behind the enemy lines. The CIC teams have lists of all known enemy agents in the theater including descriptions and personalities.

The work of CIC has changed greatly since the initial landings in Africa. In Africa the teams were called security detachments and their duties varied all the way from counterintelligence and combat intelligence to counter-espionage and even espionage. During the Sicilian operations the AMG was not yet fully organized and CIC teams were required to handle many of the normal functions of AMG. In the Italian theater, however, there are well-defined boundaries between functions of the CIC and the AMG. The two agencies cooperate closely but all organization of local governments is handled entirely by the AMG. Punishment for infractions of restrictions placed upon local residents by CIC or AMG is meted out by the AMG courts.

According to one infantry division, a total of sixty enemy agents have been apprehended in the italian theater, more than in any other theater in action. Of this sixty , thirteen agents have been apprehended by the CIC detachment of this division. For a period of approximately two months this division had the largest frontage of any division in the theater as well as fifteen miles of seafront. These agents were caught attempting to filter through our lines or to land in boats along the beach. A company from a tank destroyer battalion was used to patrol the fifteen miles of beach. This company operated continuous patrols along the beach road as well as OP's spaced at one kilometer intervals along the coast. The OP's had telephonic communication with the CIC headquarters. As soon as a boat was sighted by the northern-most OP, CIC was notified. Progress of the boat past each OP was likewise reported and, as the boat pulled in to shore, a patrol met it and rushed the occup ants to CIC headquarters. It was necessary to register all fishermen to prevent their acting as Axis agents. Permits were given the fishermen, allowing them to go not over 500 meters to sea nor more than one kilometer to the north or south of the boat dock. Should the fishermen forget and move out too far, machine gun fire across the bow of the boat quickly turned them back.

Most of the agents taken by the CIC detachment of this division were taken on the beach. They arrived in boats, usually in the company of harmless refugees who were used as a blind. They often carried radios. One group of four agents were taken 8 April 1944. As the boat neared the shore a plane passed over the boat and one of the occupants was observed to drop a radio into the sea. The four men were Italians, well-dressed in civilian clothes and carried a total of $8,000 in United States, British and Italian currency. One of the men had been directed to operate a radio station in

Naples, two of them were to operate a radio repair shop in Naples for repair of German radios and the fourth agent was to proceed to Sicily for reasons unknown.

Apprehension of agents who attempt to infiltrate in our lines by land presented a different problem. The network of roads and rivers in the division and corps sectors is too large for the assigned personnel of the detachments to cover. Therefore the Carabinieri are drafted to operate patrols and check points. The division sector is divided into two areas, a prohibited and a restricted area. The prohibited area is forward; it contains the most vital military installations which cannot be watched closely by the CIC. Movement of civilians within this area is prohibited. Civilians know that they are subject to trial if found here. Movement in the restricted area, which is to the rear of the prohibited area, is only by pass. Passes are issued by AMG after complete investigation by CIC and are issued only in extreme emergencies.

Coverage of the forward or forbidden area is maintained mostly by the combat units. Any civilian found in this area is taken back to the PW cage for processing by the CIC. In the restricted area patrols are maintained by Carabinieri mounted on bicycles or on foot. All roads leading into the area are patrolled and the river was patrolled for boats or rafts. These patrols check in periodically at MP check points. Road blocks are set up on roads which can not be patrolled and manned by Carabinieri. Thus, in order for an agent to filter through the division area, he must pass by the battalion outposts, through the front line troops, by the MP check points and forward collecting points, through the straggler line, cross the Garigliano river and avoid the Carabinieri patrols and road blocks. This security was believed to be 100% effective.

The two cardinal principles that must govern operation of a CIC detachment in a forward area are (1) rigid control of civilian movement and (2) indoctrination of our combat troops. If these two principles are followed, movement of a lone civilian or group of civilians becomes conspicuous. Immediately after occupation of a town, friendly informants are contacted and lists of local Fascists obtained. The local Podesta (mayor) is maintained in office if he is definitely known to be friendly to the Allied cause; otherwise he is jailed pending investigation, and another local man put in the office by the AMG. All local residents are registered through local town officials, separate registers made of strangers and house guests and their hosts warned that any movements of their guests are to be reported immediately. Known Fascists are thrown into jail pending investigation. Residences and offices of suspected personnel are thoroughly searched for documents, radios, undue amounts of money, weapons, etc., which might indicate that they are agents.

Personnel of the CIC detachments will do well to learn the local language, as this is much more satisfactory than the use of interpreters. Masses of refugees must be screened in the apprehension of a few agents. The Germans have a system of releasing refugees to screen the movement of agents. In one instance, 500 refugees were released to cover the movement of ten agents into one corps sector. All ten were apprehended. All refugees entering our lines are screened. First they are stripped and searched for weapons, documents and money. Agents usually carry from $200 to $5,000 in cash supplied by the Germans. The younger and more intelligent looking men and women are most likely prospects. All are interrogated by CIC personnel. Those who excite suspicion as possible agents are given special attention. Those who passed through German military zones and seem to have information of a tactical nature are turned over to the IPW team for interrogation. All personnel not falling into these two categories are turned over to the FSS (Field Security Section) for processing and evacuation.

Once an agent has been apprehended by the CIC, he is held in custody pending preparation of the charges against him. Charges are prepared by the CIC, confessions almost invariably obtained and all evidence assembled. The agent is then turned over to a General Allied Military Court for trial.

German agents are trained by three espionage agencies: General Staff Intelligence (Ic), Intelligence Service of the OKW (Abwehr), and Sicherheitsdienst (S.D.). The Abwehr, which trains most of the agents employed in the Italian theater, has not been too successful in training Italians. They seem to be trying to make up in quantity what they lack in quality, sending out 100 agents in hopes that five will get through and accomplish their mission.

CIC OPERATIONS ON LEYTE

For the first time in SWPA operations, Leyte presented an opportunity for CIC to operate in the manner for which it was designed. To perform its share of the counterintelligence mission CIC had detachments with division, corps, and many headquarters, plus an additional "area" detachment under the army detachment commander. In contrast to comparatively primitive and scattered peoples previously encountered, Leyte's population of approximately a million intelligent and civilized inhabitants, influenced by several years of Japanese administration and propaganda, offered real problems of collaboration and potential subversive activity. To cope with this situation was in itself a full time task for CIC detachments; in addition, there was greater need than ever before to assist G-2s through the interrogation of guerrillas and civilians for tactical information. The summary given below illustrates in part the changed complexion and increased scope of CIC activities which may be expected to continue throughout the Philippine campaign.

In past landings CIC interest in securing documents has been chiefly to assist in the expeditious collection of tactical information. On Leyte, however, there was urgent need to search for and secure documents of counterintelligence importance. Records of the Japanese dominated Bureau of Constabulary, of the local police, of Japanese "trading" organizations used as fronts for espionage and "pacification" and of the Kempei Tai or Jap Military Police, while without tactical significance, are potential sources of information regarding enemy agents. The division CIC detachment entering Tacloban with advanced troops, for example, took immediate steps to search and secure the most important enemy and civil installations.

The proper guarding of key buildings was difficult since troops were not available for the purpose; Filipinos pressed into service required constant supervision to see that they held their posts and prevented the entry of looters. Although coverage could not be complete, it enabled the acquisition of many documents of both tactical and counterintelligence value.

On entering towns CIC detachments invariably were met with a disorganized and bewildered populace. In cases where PCAU had not yet arrived, CIC had to establish immediate contact with responsible local citizens and do whatever was possible to assist in the re-establishment or order. Guerrillas, some bona fide and some self-styled, were usually on hand with elaborate lists of "spies" and "collaborators". In not a few cases the unfortunate suspects themselves, ranging in ages from 15 to 50, were brought in by zealous vigilantes at rifle's point. Previously compiled lists of personalities were naturally insufficient to provide immediate confirmation or denial of the allegations made by these volunteer peace officers, who were themselves the sole available witnesses and of unknown reliability. In the initial and most confused phases decisions could be based only on commonsense evaluation and close interrogation of the informant. It was soon found that the average Filipino must be pressed for specific details of when, where, how and against whom the alleged offense was committed. Later experience showed that by requesting sworn affidavits many extravagant accusations could be eliminated.

Filipinos have been detained by CIC only when believed dangerous to the security of our forces; that is willing and able to be of active assistance to the enemy, through espionage, sabotage or other subversive activity. The tactical situation has been an important factor in determining the degree of risk presented by a suspect. In forward areas it was often necessary to detain persons on meager evidence, subject to later investigation. As operations progressed and conditions in an area became more stable the necessity for physical detention diminished and more complete investigations could be made. Persons who, although wholehearted collaborators, were physically incapable, indisposed or otherwise unlikely to act as agents for the enemy could be released under restrictions after the critical phase had passed. Generally those were ordered to remain in their own barrios and to report periodically to the local police or CIC.

There was also, however, the problem of unofficial justice and "kangeroo courts" to be met. After the long Japanese occupation it was natural that those who had been fighting the Japs in the hills should be bitter towards those who had worked with the Japs in the barrios. As a typical illustration, once several armed guerrillas reported to a CIC office, saluting smartly. Asked their business, they produced a letter which began "You are hereby directed to liquidate the following traitors". On another occasion a CIC agent, the sole CIC representative in a small municipality, was presented with an unexpected emergency when a local guerrilla leader with a band of eager and well-armed followers arrived in town and commenced loading some fifty-odd terrified civilians aboard two captured trucks.

Considerable diplomacy, much argument and several bottles of "tuba" were
necessary before the guerrilla officer's demands could be revised down-
wards to three arch collaborators, these to be delivered to the nearest
MP stockade and not whisked off to the hills. Until law and order could
be firmly re-established and the local police re-organized, it was not
surprising that quite a few civilians of guilty conscience should present themselves to CIC and ask to be locked up for their own protection.

It has proved a far from simple task to establish sufficient
evidence to detain or release a suspect. Political and personal jealous-
ies colored the opinions and even the sworn statements of many informants. Those who had suffered under the occupation suspected the worst
of those who had not. Townspeople were suspicious of the farmers, and
vice versa; for, during Jap rule movement between Jap and guerrilla
zones of influence was generally difficult and sometimes dangerous.
The town dweller who wandered out into the country ran the risk of being
picked up and closely interrogated by the guerrillas as a potential agent of the Japs, while the farmer straggling into town had a good chance
of being beaten up by the Kempei Tai as a guerrilla spy. Therefore,
few people knew a great deal of what went on in other localities except
through rumor. From the guerrilla point of view those who had not
actively aided them, or those who had somehow offended them, were often
a priori collaborationists. Opinions and heresay evidence were as
plentiful as facts were elusive.

For this reason the early establishment of an informant
system was an obvious essential. The most reliable and reasonable rep-
presentatives of the loyal factions, town and guerrilla, were sought.
Wherever possible contact was established with responsible guerrilla
officers familiar with the locality and capable of separating spiteful
allegations from those which were serious. In the towns likely informants included the priest, town officials prior to the surrender, particularly the justice of the peace, school teachers, business men and
others with intelligence, a sense of civic responsibility, and close
contact with local affairs. Once this preliminary groundwork had
been accomplished, names of suspects could be submitted to the members
of this informal "panel" in turn. If they had personal knowledge of a
suspect's activities during the occupation and cleared him of the
charges, the need for an exhaustive investigation was obviated.

"Collaborator" and "Pro-Japanese" were terms applied so in-
discriminately by informants to those whom they distrusted or disliked
that they had little counterintelligence meaning. A BC who had betrayed
and tortured guerrillas was a collaborator, but so was the woman who
cooked for the Kempei Tai, the man appointed by the Japs to a minor
position, the girl who lived with a Jap officer. Many cases reported
to CIC consisted of petty crimes committed without interference from
the military, such as stealing from the house of a guerrilla. Many
were suspect ex-officio: the BC, the mayor, the city official. Many
were opportunists, working with the Japs for money or position. CIC
was concerned only when the degree and character of association, together with collateral information, suggested that persons might continue to serve the enemy if given the opportunity.

The investigation and disposition of collaborationists, as such, have been left to the appropriate agencies of the Philippine Commonwealth Government.

Although cooperation with the Japs prior to our arrival has not been considered grounds in itself for detention, it should obviously be held a bar to civic office. CIC has accordingly worked closely with PCAU in the re-establishment of civil government. Persons tentatively selected for municipal positions are first referred to CIC for clearance, which is normally accomplished through the informant panel. The early organization of police agencies is of particular concern to counter-intelligence. The general procedure has been for the chief of municipal police, selected with CIC approval, to nominate police personnel who will in turn be screened. Former BC members have been avoided. The Philippine Constabluary, being the equivalent of a state police force, was re-activated by the provincial government in a similar manner. Once functioning, these agencies proved of great assistance in implementing security measures.

To guard against the attempt of enemy agents to enter or leave our lines, security controls were instituted on both the north-east and west coasts of Leyte. On the west coast Filipino beach controls interrogated all persons arriving by water and restricted those of unknown loyalty coming from Cebu or other enemy occupied areas. In San Juanico Straits CIC cooperated with the US Navy and Philippine Army personnel in the establishment of a water patrol to check all civilian craft crossing into Leyte.

CIC with forward elements screened refugees entering our lines as thoroughly as the situation would permit. Persons with tactical information of value to the immediate command were interrogated on the spot, the results being forwarded at once to the G-2. Those whose knowledge comprised areas farther advanced were passed back wherever possible to the headquarters concerned. In this manner much valuable information of immediate and future operational areas was obtained. At the same time suspicious individuals discovered coming into US controlled areas were detained pending investigation. Guerrilla representatives greatly facilitated the interrogation and classification of suspects.

As a result of CIC's close contact with civilians and guerrillas, the function of liaison with guerrilla units was delegated by many division G-2s to their CIC detachments. In all cases CIC worked closely with those who coordinated guerrilla affairs, a cooperation which proved mutually beneficial. As previously observed, guerrilla blacklists cannot be taken at face value; personal conversation with guerrilla leaders, however, has produced much definite information concerning enemy and collaborationist personalities and organizations.

Japanese intelligence agencies existing on Leyte at the time of our landing appear to have been principally concerned with anti-guerrilla measures. Japanese trading firms were used for this purpose, as were the Bureau of Constabulary detachments throughout the island. In addition to these, the Kempei Tai established its own informer system, known locally as the Ju Tai.

Composed largely of boys too young to realize the seriousness of their actions, this organization acted as the eyes and ears of the Jap MPs, informing them when guerrillas came into the towns and acting as guides on mopping up operations.

Among the more interesting cases handled by CIC to date is that of a prominent police officer of pre-war days who was continued in office by the Japs. To the guerrillas and other loyal factions he explained that he kept his job to act as a buffer between them and the military administration. Throughout the occupation he managed to please both sides, gaining the confidence of the guerrillas as well as a promotion from the Japs. After our landing he was selected to retain his office, including his Jap-conferred promotion. His energy, military bearing and organizational ability marked him as an efficient leader and executive.

While keeping him under close but unobtrusive observation, CIC investigation uncovered considerable confirmation of these qualities, if not of the officer's loyalty. The division CIC detachment which first entered the town had prudently secured all records from the police headquarters. Censorship uncovered further correspondence of his department. These records disclosed the existence of an elaborate organization of "secret agents", each of whom reported by number on guerrilla and pro-American activities. This was not in itself conclusive, for if the officer had expurgated the reports of his agents he would have been keeping his promise to assist the guerrillas. The discovery of further documents, however, enabled a comparison of reports received from agents and those submitted by the officer to the Japanese; nothing had been omitted. With the reports as foundation, interrogation of the agents themselves added further evidence of his duplicity. Before the investigation was completed it was found that he had dismissed operatives for failure to apprehend a high guerrilla leader who had personally vouched for the officer's loyalty. So confident was the officer of his position that when he suddenly found himself incarcerated in his own jail he had neglected to destroy further damaging evidence in the form of diaries and personal records.

All these activities emphasized the need for CIC detachments to be mobile and flexible. Whereas in earlier operations CIC personnel were allocated to regimental, division and corps CPs, now the innumerable problems connected with the civilian population required that sub-offices be established in principal towns. Messing arrangements were improvised to enable the bulk of CIC personnel to operate where the need was greatest. When division detachments had to displace forward on short notice as the command itself advanced, corps detachment commanders had to be ready to take over and continue to operate the offices established by divisions. Similarly, the army detachment, using its own personnel or the area personnel attached to it, relieved corps detachments of responsibility in rear areas. Experience gained in keeping up-to-date files of reports, suspects and informants made it possible to effect these transfers without interrupting the flow of activity.

Leyte has given CIC its biggest job t but bigger tasks are yet to come. It is perhaps initial landing in the Philippines was made here, indanao or Luzon with their greater populations a Japanese civilians; for all the experience gained o needed to accomplish the CIC mission in future opera

Leyte has given CIC its biggest job to date in this theater, but bigger tasks are yet to come. It is perhaps fortunate that our initial landing in the Philippines was made here, rather than in indanao or Luzon with their greater populations and large numbers of Japanese civilians; for all the experience gained on Leyte will be needed to accomplish the CIC mission in future operations.